ENLARGING
Our Comfort Zones

A Life of Unexpected Destinations

Craig K. Comstock

BOOKS & OTHER MAJOR PUBLICATIONS
by Craig K. Comstock

Worse Than Futile: The Loyalty Provision of the National Defense Education Act, with foreword by Senator John F. Kennedy (a stand-alone report published by the *Harvard Crimson*, 1960)

Sanctions for Evil: Sources of Social Destructiveness, with Nevitt Sanford (a book first published by Jossey-Bass, Inc., 1971; paperback edition by Beacon Press, 1972)

Faculty Development in a Time of Retrenchment, a report on behalf of the Group for Human Development in Higher Education, of which the author was a member (published by Change Magazine Press, 1974)

Citizen Summitry: Keeping the Peace When It Matters Too Much to Be Left to Politicians, with Don Carlson (a book published by Jeremy P. Tarcher, Inc., 1986)

Securing Our Planet: How to Succeed When Threats Are Too Risky and There's Really No Defense, with Don Carlson (a book published by Jeremy P. Tarcher, Inc., 1986)

Global Partners: Citizen Exchange with the Soviet Union (a book published by Ark Communications Institute, 1987)

The Elmwood Quarterly, founded and edited by Craig K. Comstock (a journal published by the Elmwood Institute, with special issues in 1992–93 on "redefining wealth," global population, eco-literacy, and deep ecology)

Gift of Darkness: Growing up in Occupied Amsterdam by Craig Comstock with foreword by Francis Weller (a book published by Willow Press, 2015)

ENLARGING
Our Comfort Zones

A Life of Unexpected Destinations

Craig K. Comstock

WILLOW PRESS   ASHLAND, OREGON

Enlarging Our Comfort Zones: A Life of Unexpected Destinations
Craig K. Comstock

© 2016 by Craig K. Comstock
Published in 2016 by Willow Press, Ashland, Oregon

All rights reserved. No part of this book may be reproduced or transmitted in any form or by any means, electronic or mechanical, including photocopying, recording, or by an information storage and retrieval system—except by a reviewer, who may quote brief passages in a review to be printed in a magazine, newspaper, or on a website—without permission in writing from the publisher.

Cover and book design: Chris Molé, Book Savvy Studio
Copy editing and proofreading: Deborah Mokma

Credits:
Cover photo: © Giulia Squillace, Stocksy.com

page 3: "Thanksgiving" (detail), a painting by the author

page 39: Cover of *Motherpeace* by Vicki Noble

page 65: Drawing of Philip Glass, © Chuck Close, courtesy of the Pace Gallery

page 69: Photo by Kani Comstock of the author, taken during the period described in this book.

page 105: Cover of *Citizen Summitry*, edited by Carlson & Comstock

page 123: Reagan & Gorbachev in Red Square, 1988 by Federal Government [Public domain], via Wikimedia Commons

Publisher's Cataloging-in-Publication
(Provided by Quality Books, Inc.)

Comstock, Craig K., 1939- author.
　Enlarging our comfort zones / Craig K. Comstock.
　pages cm
　Includes bibliographical references and index.
　ISBN 978-0-9967044-0-3

　1. Self-actualization (Psychology)　I. Title.

BF637.S4C6526 2016　　　　158.1
　　　　　　QBI16-600051

ISBN: 978-0-9967044-0-3
10 9 8 7 6 5 4 3 2 1

This book describes the experience of the author and others in various practices, projects, situations, and workshops, but is not a recommendation to anybody else to try these or similar activities. The author invites readers to consider enlarging their comfort zones, but assumes no liability for particular actions.

Dedication

*To the clients and friends
who led me into new worlds
and to readers who risk
enlarging their comfort zones*

Contents

Introduction xi

ONE WAY OUT OF A COMFORT ZONE
   1 | Wake-up Calls 1
   2 | The Transition 23

SOME ADVENTURES
   3 | A Tantric Initiation 49
   4 | A Glorious Surprise 59
   5 | Family Dynamics 83

HELPING A LITTLE TO END A WAR
   6 | Ark 101
   7 | Meeting the Other Side 121

AN INVITATION
   8 | Openness to Experience 145

     Appendix | Scenarios 151
Notes 171
Index 187
Acknowledgments 191
About the Author 193

Good musicians ... can easily absorb other influences and make [them] organically their own so that new influences are embedded, so there's the process of constant growth, and then finally ... [are] able to transfer ... all of their knowledge and give it to somebody else so they can actually look at the world and figure it out for themselves.... So it's a process of birth, it's a process of constant cultural re-birth.

> – YO-YO MA,[1] interviewed by Krista Tippett
> on radio show, "On Being"

Introduction

How do we learn to enlarge our comfort zones instead of lapsing into a life of habit? How do we negotiate the awkward stage of trying something new and learn to operate there?[2]

This book is the story of ten years of a challenging, surprising, and deeply satisfying career that gave me the repeated opportunity to create an expanded comfort zone. It starts with a life falling apart around the age of forty, and describes the happy discoveries this allowed.

The period included an initiation into tantra, a spontaneous "spiritual experience," an intensive workshop about patterns learned in my family of origin, and then initiatives to help end the Cold War with the USSR. Along the way, we meet strong women, a teacher of sexual enhancement, the founder of an influential and powerful workshop, a multi-millionaire entrepreneur, and a pioneer of "citizen diplomacy."

As a former director of the William James Center for Adult Development,[3] I gradually learned to find what my friend Bill Kauth[4] calls the "gold" in all this, without being overwhelmed by the bulk of the ore. Lots of people fall into divorces, or lose parents, or suffer reversals in their careers, or have road accidents—we feel grief but, the question is, what do we do next?[5]

Happiness is threatened by not only by collapse, but also by what psychologists call "hedonic adaptation,"[6] a phrase that describes the fading of pleasure as we get used to having got what we thought we wanted. I had the luck to become a book creation coach, working with authors who wanted to write their own books, but who sought a little help up the learning curve. This practice put me in touch with many creative people, especially on the West Coast.

One of the happiest moments in this career came when I wandered into an unfamiliar bookstore and browsed the table with a sign, "recommended by our staff."[7] There were about sixty books. Spotting known covers, I realized that a quarter of them were by my clients.

Because these clients wanted to reach an audience of general readers, they valued my naïve questions about their special knowledge: At first I could ask about things that were obvious to them. But to continue helping clients, I had to be initiated into the worlds they represented. As this memoir reveals in detail, this wrenched me out of my comfort zone, not once but repeatedly.

We each create a comfort zone, an area in which we know how to operate, are not startled, feel at home. Some of us keep the initial adult comfort zone for life. That's fine with me. Constructing a comfort zone is a huge achievement, not to be lightly tampered with. For others of us, however, we seek to enlarge the existing comfort zone. This usually means a period of awkwardness, perhaps of wariness, as we learn the ways of the new addition.

Some of us seek to enlarge our comfort zones out of boredom. Some are pulled out by the demands of a job. Some people discover they want to return to an interest or ambition abandoned some time ago. Some are introduced to a new world by a love relationship or other friend.

Can that period of awkwardness be made any safer, shorter, or smoother? Some of us have mentors who help. Some people have to meet an emergency, helped in some cases by professionals. Some keep part of what they have been doing while also exploring a new world. There are many patterns, including the ones illustrated here.

Expanding one's comfort zone can become a way of life, a habit based on curiosity and what psychologists call "openness to experience."[8] We all know people who never change and others who seek to master things they don't know quite how to do. There are wonderful people at both extremes. This book focuses on the practice of venturing out.

In form it is both a self-help book and a memoir of a period in my own life and of people whom I met and in some cases with whom I worked during a decade. As a book creation coach, working with authors who wanted to write their own books, I was often led into new worlds, the worlds that they knew and in many cases about which they taught workshops, and into which they were seeking to initiate readers. I was the beneficiary of their wisdom, often after an initial struggle to absorb it.

GOING THROUGH CUSTOMS

My goal is to make it a little easier to expand our comfort zone, in part by describing my own struggles, in part by exploring what helped others to grow. Above all, I hope to convey the adventure of where the process can lead. For example, after taking a plane to Moscow, I once anxiously opened my suitcase for an already stern-looking customs official, revealing forty copies of a new book, *Citizen Summitry*.[9]

This was in late 1986, an uneasy time in that totalitarian state. Almost nobody then foresaw that the Cold War would ever end. In April of that year, the nuclear power station at Chernobyl had exploded. (The plant was located in Ukraine, then a province of the USSR.) In October the Reykjavik summit meeting between Gorbachev and Reagan, in Iceland, had ended abruptly. It was not a good time to be bringing a cache of books into a closed country. There in the entry area of Sheremetyevo International Airport, the customs inspector called over his uniformed boss.

Fortunately, the book, which I had co-edited, contained thanks to the Vice-President of the Soviet Academy of Sciences plus some Soviet contributions that he had helped us to obtain, plus a dramatic ink drawing of a TV "space-bridge" between Moscow and San Francisco. After looking at all this, the colonel smiled and said, "I understand: your country, my country, peace," and he waved me in.

An interviewer and crew from All-Soviet TV were waiting for me, perhaps because of the novelty of a Westerner who was neither a Cold Warrior nor a "useful idiot," to use, as I did in the interview, Lenin's pungent term for a Westerner who could be trusted to parrot the party line. In contrast, my co-editor Don Carlson and I had invited various Soviets to envision, together with Americans, the end of the Cold War between us (or at least that very dangerous version of it).

In one sense, this book is about how I got to that place. Although the wake-up calls in my early forties felt dismal at the time, they gave me the opportunity to venture outside my comfort zone and adopt a profession that kept initiating me into new worlds. Unlike the work on the Cold War, most of these worlds were not political, but they prepared me for at least a small role in helping to meet a challenge that seemed impossible.

What I want to do is illustrate the process, in at least one life, of successively enlarging a comfort zone. The process can bring value beyond anything imagined in advance, but it usually involves a stage of awkwardness, uncertainty, confusion.

For example, I had reached early middle age with a well-defined comfort zone, and probably would have stayed safely inside it if not for a series of shocks. These events freed me to develop a new career and thus the opportunity of a second chance, after having happily taught, directed research, and been a well-paid consultant and co-author[10] of a book (*Sanctions for Evil: Sources of Social Destructiveness*).

Many people suffer worse shock. For example, I did not have a serious illness, an addiction, loss of a fortune, or a devastating accident. But a moderate loss can, with luck and a helpful attitude, lead to unexpected gains.

A LITTLE OUTSIDE

At the foundation where I worked within the decade of this brief memoir, one of my colleagues responded to a proposal by saying, gently, "that's a little outside my comfort zone." She spoke the way that aghast but courteous people in the South initially seem to agree that we "might could" do something, actually meaning, however, "we could go that way if we didn't have a much better idea."

The phrase "comfort zone" started me thinking about the areas we all define where we know how to act and can more or less succeed. At the foundation starting in 1984 we had the single goal of trying to help end the Cold War as it then existed, which required, as my thoughtful colleague knew, operating often in gray areas or in activities that we didn't know would work.

Almost all of the stories in this book are drawn from little more than a decade of my life, 1981-92. After a transition, they tell of being drawn into worlds unknown to me, sometimes with skepticism or reluctance, and then of finding, inside these worlds, treasures that I'd never even imagined. This is an adventure story,[11] of discovering some of the hidden worlds that exist all around us, ordinarily never entered or even seen. I illustrate this process with some stories almost entirely from my forties, but it's as much about other people as about me; about mentors, friends, co-workers. (Some of the units carry the story outside the chronological order of this book, after which the next unit returns to that order.)

A few words of context and gratitude: I began adult life with huge advantages: a childhood with a close family in the suburbs of New York City, education at Harvard College and other "elite" institutions, a fellowship for travel abroad, a loving, bright, and adventurous wife who'd graduated from the same university.

Later, after the transition described here, I overheard a former college roommate trying to answer a question from his son, "what does Craig do?" Fumbling for an answer, this distinguished professor was vague but kind: "he helps people." He was referring to my early work as a "book creation coach."

What I want to describe is the passage from initial confusion and resistance to the discovery of worlds of which I probably would have remained unaware, had I not been asked to "help." And I want to celebrate some of the unsung heroes with whom I had the good fortune to work.

FOR WHOM?

Within a given level of genetic endowment, it is curiosity and the habit of learning[12] that determine working intelligence. If one can identify more with finding out than with knowing, if one can live with the anxiety of not having mastered something (yet), he or she can make full use of whatever mental powers that person has.

I love the story of a child telling his father about a success. The parent congratulates him and adds, "be sure to tell me also about enterprises at which you fail." His point was that if we always succeed, we may not be exploring widely enough. This father was teaching a kind of courage, which is not fearlessness, but deliberate persistence in the face of natural anxiety.

My dad's mother, a frontier schoolteacher, often said, "well, I've never heard that before," almost as if to doubt the credentials of the unfamiliar. As a young person, I thought, "what kind of a life is it in which any novelty is worthy of comment, as if everything otherwise is familiar?" When I grew up, I wanted to be a person who said, "Do I know? Not yet. Tell me about it. Show me. Help me do it."

So this is a book about learning, not so much mastering the details of a known sphere, which of course is necessary, as of entering new spheres, of exploring. As an adolescent I began to notice that many discoveries are made by people for whom the field of discovery is a second field. (To mention only one example, the discovery of the structure of DNA.) As a young adult, I noticed that some firms have succeeded in part by deliberately mixing people up and encouraging conversations between disparate kinds of experts. A tiny minority of these encounters led to basic and perhaps very profitable discoveries. (Apple and Google know this, as do many firms in information technology.)

"Openness to experience" is almost the opposite of "authoritarian personality," a concept described by one of my mentors, the psychologist Nevitt Sanford. (With colleagues, he wrote the book of that name.) He was not a traditional thinker. After one long meeting in his office, about starting a new school within what had thus far been solely a research institute, the champion of this proposal suggested appointing a feasibility committee. It would report in six months. Nevitt said, "we might could do that or," and here he drew on his pipe and blew a smoke ring, "we could start the school tomorrow morning."

He and I wrote the prospectus before dinner and the next day he and other leading psychologists and psychotherapists phoned colleagues in colleges, described the prospectus, and asked them to tell their best seniors about it. We had the first applications within a few days. More than forty years later, the Wright Institute is accredited and widely known in its field.

Openness to experience is related to "absorption," which can be defined as total attention. Though it comes from a separate research tradition, "flow"[13] is related to attending totally, to forgetting everything other than the immediate challenge, which might be climbing a rock face, performing brain surgery, or playing jazz. This kind of absorption is self-guided and serves as its own reward, or as some psychologists say, it's "autotelic."

COLLAPSE AND TRANSITION

In my case, I was helped by two factors, first by a collapse of the life that I had developed, then by a series of good, not to say wonderful, new kinds of experience. I don't want anyone to suffer a collapse, which may have been necessary in my case. (I am told that in Alcoholics Anonymous, many new recruits come only when they have reached "rock bottom.") I didn't have any of the obvious addictions, except perhaps to what I knew, at various stages, as normality. Which, however, may be a strong fixation.

The collapse can be briefly told in the first chapter, while the second shows some of the values by which I was guided in building a new kind of life. Then the rest of the book is about venturing beyond my comfort zone and thus discovering worlds that I did not know existed and, looking back, am happy that I was initiated into.

The transition, however, can feel startling. While living in North Africa, I once visited ruins of a Roman city in the desert, an ancient city that looked as if it had just been evacuated, intact but lonely. Nobody was on the ancient streets. People were elsewhere, in the nearby contemporary city of Souk-el-Arba in the west of Tunisia. I wandered into a dark stone Roman house (no windows), and was reflecting on a civilization that assumed it would never die. Here I was, alone in the ruins.

As my eyes began to adjust to the murk inside the windowless building, I was startled by the sound of something dropped, then by the realization that there were other people in the large room, men in robes, two horizontal circular millstones, and a donkey that would pull a pole and thus turn the top stone. A man was dropping olives through a hole in the stone. I was doubly startled, not only because I had assumed I was alone, but also because the scene could have existed in the bible pictures that I'd studied as a child in Sunday school.

I greeted the men in the few words of the local language that I then knew, and they mumbled back, almost as if I belonged there. After a few moments, as calmly as possible, I left and walked back to the car and the world that I knew, but filled with curiosity about the life that I had glimpsed and about which I learned more during a year in North Africa.

Many of us stumble or venture out of an established comfort zone once, but this is a book about enlarging your comfort zone as a style of life. Finding a comfort zone is a tremendous achievement. With luck, your partner is there, your work, your very identity. The trouble is, the zone may become a little boring or constrained. You may be reminded of other parts not yet developed. Then you have a choice of making the best of your present condition, or, while respecting others, enlarging your comfort zone. You put yourself in new situations, you enter unfamiliar worlds, you learn a broader view.

Along the way, I give as much attention to some of the amazing people whom I met on this path, with some of whom I had the honor of working. They were typically people who grew out of one career into another, people who paid attention to more than one field, people who sought to serve, people who took on challenges said to be impossible. I'm sure that I missed a lot of what these people had to teach, but I learned what I could and try to pass along the lessons here.

BEYOND MERITOCRACY

In the meritocracy, we learn to build a resume and to enter a monoculture of success. One of my early mentors, the sociologist David Riesman,[14] weary of all the Cold War talk about the need for leaders to avoid a "failure of nerve," inverted the phrase and praised the "nerve of failure," the willingness to try something even if it might fail. Why? Because it might succeed in a surprising way, and because if it failed you would have to learn resilience. In some cases, as I would discover, the difficult and uncertain effort was inescapable because, if it failed, nothing else would matter.

I want to celebrate the willingness to pass through recurrent periods of initiation, those times when we feel like stumbling in dense fog through a field of birch saplings. Everything is white and we realize we are lost, almost clueless. Perhaps we hear some ambiguous sounds. Then, sometimes, the sun breaks through, and we can see how to get to the brook that we have heard. But for a while we stumble, with no guarantees that the fog will ever lift. The very good news is that once we learn how to tolerate uncertainty, we can have the opportunity to discover something new, possibly wonderful, beyond our dreams.

And who knows? The future may throw us into a fog, in which case the best preparation would be the experience of having entered the fog voluntarily and thriving.

One Way Out of the Comfort Zone

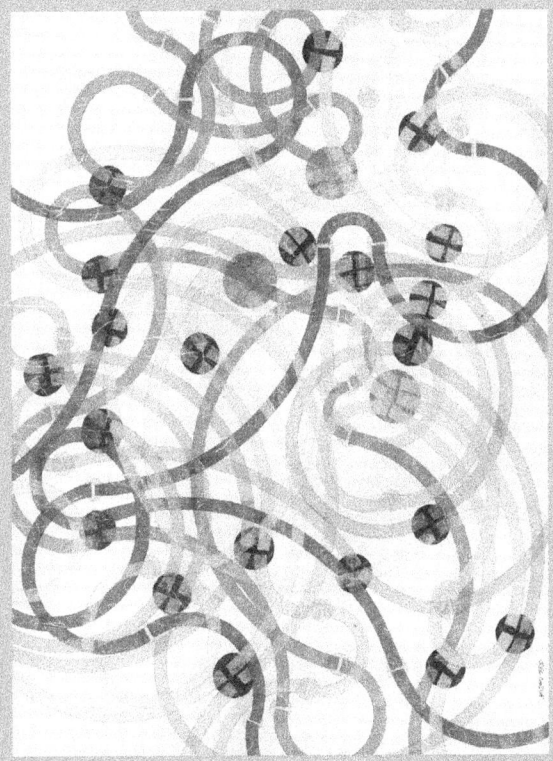

Washi Arcs collage by author

1

Wake-Up Calls

In 1981 my parents invited their children who were living nearby to a Thanksgiving feast in the house to which they had retired, in Santa Rosa, just north of the San Francisco Bay Area. Three of the kids drove up together.

Everything seemed normal. My mother was in the kitchen in a house much more modern than the Dutch-colonial-style place in which we had been raised in the Northeast. "Can you help by grinding the cranberry sauce?" Mom asked me. I knew that her recipe involved combining the tart red spheres with a navel orange (rind and all) plus walnuts and sherry. "Okay, where's the meat grinder?" I was set up with the ingredients, a big bowl, and an old zinc-plated grinder with its S-curved handle. My sister Kani was helping with the turkey, and the youngest sibling, Barbara, was cooking vegetables. Dad was helping to set the table. Then he stepped into the kitchen and surprised me with an urgent request.

THE QUESTION

"Could you go outside with me and help round up the sheep?" At first I was puzzled. We were among streets full of houses in the California town where the botanist Luther Burbank had settled. In the salubrious climate, there were many plants growing in gardens, but no livestock in town. Where were the sheep? "Please help me," said Dad, "we have to get the sheep to the railway station." Santa Rosa may have had an old railway station, but trains no longer came through. And in any case, why were we suddenly responsible for a herd of sheep?

Perhaps Dad was setting up one of his jokes. "If I went outside," I cautiously replied, "would I see the sheep?" "Of course," said Dad, "and if we don't herd them quickly, they may get away." Then he added the line that tipped me off. "It's strange," he said, "that Minnesota has moved so close that it's just over the hill." He waved toward a California slope that we called "golden" in the late autumn (and visitors from the East just regarded as clad with burnt stubble).

My Dad had grown up in southern Minnesota, on a farm where his father *did* keep sheep. Suddenly his words made sense, but the sense they made was that either we'd slipped into *The Wizard of Oz* or he'd become delusional.

I assured him that any sheep would be taken care of and that we could meanwhile sit down to Thanksgiving dinner. More than his death years later, this was the moment when, for me, the floor fell away. I took the other members of the family aside and told them what had happened. The table talk was somewhat subdued, but it usually consisted initially of little more than murmurs of appreciation for the roasted "bird" and the other special foods, with perhaps some allusion to the Pilgrims.

Later, after we had heard a tentative medical diagnosis of Alzheimer's Syndrome,[1] my mother retrospectively claimed that she had discerned some earlier signs, but the exact nature of the dementia remained unclear: only an autopsy, we were told, would provide certainty.

But the symptoms grew more and more pronounced.

detail of painting, "Thanksgiving," by the author

While Dad remained good-natured for the most part, he became "forgetful," making careful lists of what he needed to do, then signs to remind him of the existence of the lists and where to find them. Forgetting the signs he had posted, he would wander off and go to sleep, during the day, on the front lawns of strangers, and when brought home by police who learned the address from his wallet, he would deny the house was his, and even say about the worried woman on the porch, "she's not my wife."

While my mother was left to deal with her long-time partner, we kids also felt abandoned, as by a death. Dad was no longer there to go to for advice, or even to complain about. The face looked like his, and the voice sounded like his, but he was living in a different mental world. Did he feel bewildered or did things seem normal to him?

With the couple living alone, Mom had to deal with all of his bizarre and sometimes frightening behavior, including his climb up a ladder onto the flat roof to check the condition of the tar. How do you safely get down a man weighing much more than you who, at times, would lose his balance even inside the house and have to lean against a wall?

My sister Kani and I decided to give Mom a little rest, so we volunteered to stay with Dad while she went off to Yosemite with another woman from her real estate office. After my stint of just sixteen hours I was ready for a vacation. (A contemporary book for caregivers was called *The 36 Hour Day*.)

During my stay with Dad in Santa Rosa, the phone rang and while I was distracted, he made his way outside. I didn't notice until he was turning the corner at the far end of the block, heading toward a busy road. Running after him, I caught up and walked beside him as if joining his expedition, and then tried to turn him around so we could go back to the house.

When he struggled against my arm around his waist, a car stopped abruptly across the road and a trembling and brave woman about my age emerged with a baseball bat. I realized that she thought I was mugging a helpless old man, and so I called out just a few words, "my father, Alzheimer's." Similarly terse, she simply said, "my mother," lowered the bat, and returned to her vehicle.

When things got even worse, Kani and I looked for a nursing home that would accept Alzheimer patients, that was affordable, and that was not depressing. What I most recall was a roomful of dazed, pasty, old folks with wheelchairs oriented toward a wall-mounted TV, and institutional meals being clicked onto metal tables, while someone mopped the hall with strong-smelling disinfectant.

We finally found an acceptable nursing home in Ann Arbor, Michigan, where our brother Bruce lived, and our mother decided to move. She would buy a small house, and Dad would live in the nursing "facility" where she visited him every day.

He was almost asked to leave the nursing home. I suppose the immediate cause was his pulling down an entire wall of draperies and personalizing some furniture. But the home managed to restore the things and he stayed.

The last time that I visited from the West Coast, he and I met in the "music room." It immediately became obvious that he had no idea who I was. I was hurt and resentful for a few seconds and didn't know what to do. Then I realized it was a big opportunity. All my life I had heard that Dad was affable with strangers, able to talk with anyone. This was my chance to see how he behaved with someone he didn't know.

We talked about this and that, until I heard myself hesitantly saying that while everyone would be sorry when he was no longer around, he didn't need to hang on for the sake of others, out of a sense of paternal duty; he could call an end when *he* wanted, as soon or as far away as he felt was right. While I was saying this, I felt as if I were a hang glider inflating my nylon wing, turning around, and running off a mountain side, as Bruce would later do. What business did I have giving somebody permission to stop worrying about other people?

A tear dripped down my cheek. The last physical contact between us was Dad reaching over and, with the back of a hand, wiping away my tear. I don't know if he would have done that with a stranger. It really didn't matter.

I was back in California when he died. I had flown from the Bay Area to Los Angeles to appear, with my book partner, on a TV show to promote ways to help end the Cold War. Weary, I checked into the hotel late at night, dropping my clothes on a chair by dim light from the bathroom, and went quickly to sleep. Before sunrise the phone rang. I heard Mom's voice: "He's gone."

Still lying down, barely awake. I turned on the bedside lamp. Floating about a dozen feet above me, I saw a figure who could almost have been my father. By the time I'd replied briefly to Mom, I realized the Hollywood hotel room had a mirror mounted on the ceiling above the bed. The figure up there was my own. I got up, had breakfast with my co-editor, and we took a cab to a TV studio.

The last act took place in Michigan where my brother, a hot air balloon pilot (and manufacturer), took us up to scatter Dad's ashes. Lit by the setting sun, the ashes flared out in a diamond shape above farmers' fields. We felt this was an appropriate place because it was near where Dad had died, and because, before an adulthood in the New York suburban area, he'd grown up on a midwest farm.

I'd attended only one funeral or memorial service before that day and, never having been in combat, had almost no experience of death except for watching autopsies as part of a volunteer program in college. Then, as a reward for transferring tissue samples in paraffin from decaying cardboard boxes to plastic bags, we were invited to join medical students in watching bodies professionally deconstructed by physicians. The age of eighteen is perhaps a little early for this experience, though young soldiers sometimes see much worse.

I did not have a choice about whether to walk through the door of my Dad's dementia. The only alternative would have been to keep a distance, but our family had always been close. As millions know, the gradual loss of a parent or friend is hard. Not recognizing his own children was a late detail in a slow deterioration. I wondered, as the process unfolded, what did he know? In particular, did he understand his own loss of faculties, or did something shield him from knowledge of his own condition?

OTHER LIFE-WORLDS

In trying to imagine Dad's experience after the dementia became obvious to us, I kept watching for hints in what he said and did. But it was only later, on the Big Island of Hawaii, that I confronted in any depth how hard it is to imagine other life-worlds.[2] On a sunny New Years Day I was sitting with a friend on a lanai (porch) overlooking Kealakekua Bay, facing toward a slope that showed the angle of cooling lava, and the rippling water between that slope and our lanai.

My friend was practicing the didgeridoo, an Australian instrument made from a hollow branch with beeswax around the upper rim. We were watching spinner dolphins[3] leap up as kayaks occasionally went across the bay from the parking field to a monument that had been erected to Captain Cook, the first European to land in these parts.

"What do you suppose the dolphins do when they're not leaping?" asked my friend as he took a rest from blowing into the didgeridoo and producing a mournful rumble. In the water, or so I had read in books, the dolphins ate, played, mated, and communicated. They subsisted on raw fish. They lived in pods. They had large brains. When dolphins were newborn, they sucked milk from their mothers' bodies, much as many human babies do.

Occasionally, I imagined, the dolphins would see humans in the water with flippers and scuba gear, blowing bubbles, curious about fish and coral. I guessed that the dolphins could see the hulls of boats with propellers that churned, and of kayaks with paddles that splashed on alternate sides.

You can know all this (it isn't much), and still have a very hard time imagining what it's like to live almost wholly in a different medium, to make nothing, have no "jobs," need nothing except some fish to eat and each other to swim and play with. Were the dolphins conscious of stars? To what extent were they ruled by instinct? What did their "language" allow them to say?

It occurred to me that the greatest difficulty in imagining other life-worlds arises because we are unable to forget what is so ordinary to us, so taken for granted that we hardly know we're assuming it. For example, many of us are always doing something, even greeting one another with the question, "keeping busy?" (If a human is not obviously busy, at least in the U.S., he or she is thought to be less than fully alive.)

I wondered whether, apart from finding fish to eat, dolphins are ever focused on other tasks. Or are they like the fishing captain[4] in Cabo San Lucas, Mexico, who, urged by a visiting gringo entrepreneur to take out a loan, accumulate a fleet of boats, and thus make a fortune, asked, "why would I do that?" The reply from the prosperous tourist: "so you can get rich and retire." The captain said, "then what would I do?" After a moment, they both laughed, because the answer was obvious: he would go fishing in a warm place.

What would it be like not to strive for anything? Presumably dolphins have no science, no math, no works of art, nothing we would recognize as music. Do they have an image of life of which we aren't even vaguely aware? Or even *could* be aware? Are they curious about humans or are we just strange marginal creatures moving around the edges of their world?

I was similarly frustrated in trying to imagine Dad's life-world immersed in Alzheimer's. Was he aware of the loss, or did the mental degeneration protect him from knowledge of itself? What did he think he was doing, forgetting his notes, wandering off, and finally not recognizing his own wife and kids? Was all this inexpressibly sad to him, or was he oblivious? Had he forgotten having ever been smart and caring?

YOSAL

My first response to my impending divorce had been to return to California. I flew back from New York to the San Francisco Bay Area, where I'd started a graduate program, lived in the paradise of a ranch on the peninsula looking west to the Pacific, and then co-directed a center on adult development at an independent institute founded in Berkeley by the well-known psychologist Nevitt Sanford. My thought was not to change, but to rebuild something like the life I'd had.

I re-registered at Stanford, having completed enough graduate courses for doctorates in two fields, and picked up work on an interdisciplinary dissertation in "literature and social thought." Living in Berkeley, I enjoyed the company of two of my siblings and other old friends. With a new friend, I arranged to spend the summer in Oxford, England, exchanging apartments with a don there who wanted to live in the Bay Area for a few months.

Life seemed good, but then the road toward an academic career was washed out by the sudden and unexpected death of my close friend and graduate program adviser. His name was Yosal Rogat,[5] and he is among the unsung heroes in this story.

At Stanford, Yosal and I had gravitated to each other, sharing, as we did, a rare interest in both law and "modernisms"[6] in social thought, literature and art. I was a grad student, who had left a law school in the Northeast after the first year. Half a generation older, Yosal had written about the Eichman trial and about Justice Oliver Wendell Holmes, and held a joint appointment at Stanford in the law school and the political science department. According to the memorial resolution composed by colleagues after his untimely death, he had taught, along with law school courses, "a unique seminar—which, like Yosal's mind, transcended departmental boundaries—on the idea of modernism."

When we met, Yosal was living just off the Stanford campus in a modest house and had the reputation, even at a top university, of being exceptionally brilliant as well as far-ranging. I signed up for his seminar on modernisms, a style of thought that he found in social thought (including legal writing), in poetry, and other literature. After the first few meetings, he loaned me his teaching notes for the class and encouraged me to scribble marginalia. I was astonished and flattered when, a week after I had given back the notebook, he mentioned that he'd had the pages retyped with my comments added in.

Modernism was a style of thought that had been arising and then dominant in the hundred or so years before we were studying it. At first, this style met formidable resistance, but eventually came to seem obvious. In literature, a course on modernism might include such American and European writers as T.S. Eliot, Andre Gide, James Joyce, Franz Kafka, Wyndham Lewis, Robert Musil, Ezra Pound, and Virginia Woolf; or in visual arts, Georges Braques, Paul Cezanne, and Pablo Picasso.

Stanford then allowed graduate students who wanted to earn an interdisciplinary doctorate to gather a committee of at least four professors drawn from two or more departments. Yosal agreed to chair my special degree committee, which came also from the English literature and psychology departments. Under the rubric of "social thought and literature," the program was about imagination and, more specifically, about the creative play or "ludic activity" of adults.

Having graduated from UCLA at age eighteen, Yosal had the manners of a prodigy. I don't know that he was overly impressed by raw intelligence, whatever that is, but he cared about integral thinking, which, as his colleagues noted, went wherever it was relevant to go.

Yosal had suffered a back injury, caused by a touch football game (and worsened, he said, by initial treatment). When I met him, he could lie down or walk, but not sit for long in a chair or stand in one place. He was a passionate cyclist and later got me to buy a mountain bike, a device that was new then, and ride it from San Francisco over the Golden Gate Bridge to the foot, and then to the top, of a mountain called Tamalpais. A long-distance runner at UCLA, Yosal at Stanford went on almost daily bike rides, which might even involve long trips over the hills to the Pacific and back to Palo Alto.

Yosal was a person about whom colleagues gossiped: How much pain was he suffering? What remarkable comment had he made? Would he ever, in the agricultural metaphors common in academic life, not only "break new ground" with his ideas but "harves" a book about them?

Alas, after the injury he was never able to sit still long enough to write anything much longer an article requested by the *New York Review of Books*. That article was on the neo-conservatives, so-called, and in particular, on Irving Kristol. Published in 1972, the article was a sort of early warning radar sighting of a political trend that has given us the war in Iraq and a fundamentalist GOP.

In New York Yosal had known Hannah Arendt, a German-born American political theorist who had escaped Europe during the Holocaust; and in California, he was employed in his early career by the Center for the Study of Democratic Institutions, which sought to bring diverse and progressive intellectual resources to bear on public policy.

Yosal was generous in sharing his thinking, which for his friends was less like fishing in a tranquil lake than like running a white-water river. His sense of humor was ironic, perhaps enhanced by his time at New College, Oxford. If he had been raised in the Northeast rather than the Los Angeles area, I suppose he would have been a New York intellectual. Instead, he could be found dining under big trees in the balmy climate of Palo Alto. I recall one lunch behind the campus union when a faculty visitor from the East was sighing that if he moved here he'd never get any work done. This would have amused the Nobel-prize winner at a nearby table.

With his health troubles, Yosal did not win any prizes during his years at Stanford, except for the admiration of students and other teachers who took the time to get close to him. As the writers of the memorial resolution delicately said, he was "stimulating and memorable … to those of his colleagues who knew him at his best. They will remember the conviction with which he insisted that to study law and politics was to study realms of human culture as well as bodies of doctrine and systems of behavior. They will remember the breadth of his humane learning and the lucidity of his intelligence." His writings on the nature of law, as shown in pieces on the Eichman trial and on the career of Justice Holmes, remain relevant decades after their publication.

Yosal died accidentally at the age of only 52. This occurred in 1980, a few years after I'd returned to California. I could have found a replacement as head of my interdisciplinary degree committee, but Yosal's death took the wind out of my sails, for the graduate program that I had imagined had come out of his unique seminar on modernisms. For me, his death was the end both of a delightful friendship and of my academic career.

TABLE TALK

I love to talk with one other person, preferably over food or drink. The logo for my professional services as a book creation coach was a café table with two steaming mugs. On community access TV, the set for my interview show was a small inlaid wooden octagonal table, over which I would palaver with a guest or two.

As long ago as 1981, the director Louis Malle gave us *My Dinner With Andre,* a movie consisting almost wholly of conversation over a meal. Some viewers disdain the movie because nothing happens, but to me the intense, frank and edgy conversation seems as exciting as a car chase.

Malle's movie also reminded me of my dissertation adviser, who had died unexpectedly in the previous year. Like Andre, Yosal was intense, though with some of the concerns of a law professor and polymath rather than a theatrical director.

In Malle's movie, an actor and playwright named Wallace Shawn has dinner with an old friend, Andre Gregory. Son of the longtime editor of *The New Yorker,* Shawn starred in the title role in *Vanya on 42nd Street,* a filmed performance of the Chekov play in an otherwise abandoned theater. In real life, Gregory is an actor and experimental director. About a decade before making the Malle movie, he directed his most famous production, *Alice in Wonderland;* and about five years after the movie, the premiere of a Wallace Shawn play. Shawn and Gregory collaborated on the script for *My Dinner with Andre* with the former taking the leading role.

Wally, as he's called in the movie, plays the straight man, the listener to Andre's astonishing tales. Andre talks about working with Jerzy Grotowski's so-called "poor theater" in Warsaw and in the Polish forest, and about attending a ritual involving a simulated burial on Long Island; he muses on the future of Western civilization.

Like my teacher Yosal, the character of Andre is a hypnotic talker, drawing on dashing experiences. In Yosal's case, these experiences included being seated, at a Brecht premiere in Los Angeles, between Charlie Chaplin and Yosal's boyhood friend's Dad who wrote *Citizen Kane*[7] for Orson Welles. Yes, Yosal dropped names (as I'm now doing); but he'd led a life in which this was less an act of trying to appear important than an ordinary reference.

Yosal could make quips and brief comments with the best of them, but most of his ideas, like Andre's stories in the movie, required what he called "a long runway." He could listen attentively, too, but when he was talking he needed space to pull many things together. Andre's hypnotic accounts in the movie reminded me, in their intensity, of Yosal's intellectual sallies, in which he'd draw material from legal history, political theory, modern literature, and Oxford language philosophy.

Almost anybody can be "interdisciplinary," if superficial acquaintance is acceptable. Yosal knew the fields upon which he drew. When one of his articles on Justice Holmes appeared, a brilliant judge who was working on a biography of Holmes wrote that Yosal's interpretation of the jurist had changed his own views to such an extent that he had to start over.

Another way in which Andre reminded me of Yosal

was his openness to what most people regarded as odd experiences and views. Each of them was not scared to be thought a little weird. I learned from Yosal an observation that I've seen variously attributed to Schopenhauer and (inevitably) the Dalai Lama: Every great idea goes through three stages of reception. In the first stage, mainstream opinion says the idea is so silly or wrong that it's not worth even refuting; or as a physicist once said, "not even wrong." In the second stage, as the idea gains adherents, the same observer exclaims, "we need to stop this now, before it destroys civilization!" In the third stage, if the idea's merit has become obvious, the same observer says, "well, you know, I thought of this myself five years ago."

Of course many ideas *are* silly or inconsequential, but Yosal made a practice of trying things out rather than rejecting them out of hand. He had prejudices; who doesn't? But he leaned toward a kind of playful tolerance.

The tragedy of his life was a touch football injury (a spinal displacement) that didn't heal, and that gradually wore him down. At the time of his accidental death at age 52, he was no longer the promising young man who, in the 1960s, had altered scholarly views of a totemic judge and seen the Eichmann trial from a unique perspective. As compared with an academic career that would normally have lasted another dozen years or more, he never had an opportunity to write the work that might have illumined modernist thought.

As I've said, other professors could have taken over Yosal's place as chair of my degree committee, but I had been drawn to the ad hoc program by an unusual person who was now dead at an early age (and had been distracted for a while before). My degree program fell victim to my mourning. The degree was something that I didn't carry to completion, as I did later adventures to be described here, including a pair of books, and after a gap, another couple.

In Malle's movie, Wally takes a cab home, having enjoyed the stories of his old friend but, according to the script that Mr. Shawn took the initiative in writing, being essentially unchanged. He looks forward to describing the occasion to his partner. (What Andre does, we don't see.) In contrast, I was profoundly changed by exposure to the particular intensity of Yosal.

AN ACCIDENT

Academic adviser dies, father gets Alzheimer's, marriage ends: what else could go wrong? After returning to Berkeley I decided to get a good bike rather than another car. One warm evening, after a superb dinner at a friend's restaurant, I was wheeling along a boulevard that intersects a street on which I'd once lived: a wide bike lane, not much traffic, good street-lights. I rode carelessly with only one hand on a brake lever.

When I was about to cross a street that had stop signs at that corner, as the boulevard did not, I saw at the last moment that a car was about to run the stop and might smash into me. I grabbed the right brake handle, which unfortunately was attached only to the brake on the front wheel. As the front wheel locked and the back of the bike lifted off the pavement, I was thrown over the handlebars

In my experience it's true that at moments of crisis everything can seem to slow down, as if time is normal only when we're not threatened or not otherwise paying close attention. Assessing the trajectory of my body, my eyes went to where I would land on the pavement, and in particular, to a manhole cover. As I arced through the air, I wondered melodramatically whether the little stars around the edge would be the last thing I'd ever see. It was as if I were observing myself fall.

"He landed on his right forearm and also, a bit, on the right side of his face. The car vanished. He noticed that his glasses frame was pretzeled on one side, a lens broken. Soon he discovered that he could get up and even carry his bike to the sidewalk. Dazed, he sat on the curb, unsure what damage he'd suffered."

A city bus braked to an unscheduled stop on that corner and the driver, equipped with a two-way radio, asked whether I wanted him to call an ambulance. No, I said, just call my sister, who lived nearby. Ordinarily I do not easily remember phone numbers, but hers came immediately to mind.

In a few minutes she appeared, accompanied by her husband, who was next to me as they pulled up and who, as a specialist on Tibetan culture, was accustomed to seeing colorful scenes. "Hi, Craig," he sweetly drawled. "Rick," said my sister, "get out, he's hurt, he has blood all over his face." This was an exaggeration. Apparently the blood was all on the right side, obscuring the vision out of that eye. We drove to the emergency room, and the good news began.

No, I had not lost consciousness. I had not injured my right eye. An X-ray revealed that the bone in my right cheek hadn't been broken. A noted plastic surgeon happened to stop by the hospital after a dinner party to use the phone (this was years before mobiles), and he would help me. He sewed up the gash so skillfully that it's hard to locate. My brother-in-law took a photo of me in the early morning, which he developed with colors reversed into complements so that my skin is a vivid blue. It conveys the situation perfectly.

Once the bandages were off, I regarded the incident as over. It never occurred to me that I might have a minor case of "post traumatic stress disorder." After all, I associated

PTSD with guys seeing a buddy shot to death beside them, or being blown up but not killed.

It was only after several years that I heard of a woman who did "cranial-sacral" work. By the standards of conventional western medicine, this approach is the kind of thing critiqued on "Quackwatch." It would have been no substitute for the excellent plastic surgery done right after the accident, or the antiseptic dressing. However, I'm unsure that PTSD is easily detectable by most allopathic doctors, much less regarded as treatable. If some practitioners would conclude, "it's all in your head," they would refer not to the plates of the scalp, but to fantasies in the brain.

A colleague on my college paper had gone on, after graduating from a prestigious medical school, to become famous as the bearded smiling face of alternative medicine. He made the sensible observation that Western medicine is unequaled at dealing with physical traumas, as from an accident, not so adept at healing many shocks or degenerative diseases. To the latter might be added a kind of wounding that doesn't show up on x-rays or available tests of blood, urine, or saliva.

What I learned from the bike accident was how wise it is to keep both hands on the brake pedals, not only the right; and how exhilarating it is to find that various terrible things have *not* happened. I also learned again that life could be transformed at any moment, not necessarily in a slow-moving Victorian deathbed scene, but suddenly, with little warning.

INCIDENTS IN ISCHGL

Sufis have a saying, that if you "die" to the ordinary world before you die, when you come to the end of your life you don't have to die with the fear that other people may feel.

In my twenties I had various "death exposures." They shared a common feature. In the brief time they were happening, they could have led to serious injury or even death, but as it turned out, none of these incidents caused me any physical harm or at least irreparable harm.

This is different from having prolonged pain or a diagnosis of a fatal illness, but then recovering, as several friends have done. But during each exposure, I felt quite intensely that I might not escape harm.

Two examples once occurred in a period of sixteen hours. While a research student at the London School of Economics, I took a ski vacation in western Austria, in what was then a modest village called Ischgl. Not a high-powered resort at the time, Ischgl had only one way of getting up the slope: a slippery rope lift. (This was before the era of the "top of the mountain concerts" which later brought to Ischgl such stars as Bob Dylan, Elton John, Rod Stewart, and Tina Turner, along with Bill Clinton.) We went there to learn to ski and then would collapse for late afternoon naps in rooms heated, from the corners, by *kacheloefens* (built-in ceramic wood stoves).

The first incident took place on a Saturday evening, when my roommate and I hired a horse-drawn sleigh to take us on the snow-covered road to a village at the end of the valley where a dance was being held. Suddenly in the darkness we saw a car's headlights racing toward us on the narrow road and realized we had no way of being seen. The driver of the sleigh yelled something in local dialect and we understood that a *taschenlampe* (flashlight) was somewhere under the lap blankets. On either side of the narrow road were icy walls of snow.

As it happened, we fumbled our way to and thumbed on the flashlight just in time for the driver of the car, a

Mercedes, to see it and slide by against the far wall of ice. Then the car was gone. I suppose the whole incident, from seeing oncoming headlights, and yanking off one of our lap blankets, took how long? Ten seconds? In that time a head-on collision seemed possible. We were clip-clopping along behind a dark horse, but the car was speeding toward us, as if the narrow valley road were an *autobahn*. A difficult situation, resolved with the loss of some paint from the right side of the car, I suppose, and loss of a lap blanket from the sleigh.

The second incident occurred the next morning. I awoke early and had breakfast, with the intention of taking a solitary walk down the valley. As I was about to leave the little hotel, my roommate, a young British TV producer, came down and asked me to stay a little while. I wanted to get started but agreed to have coffee with him.

As I started walking on that Sunday morning, the sky was totally blue; the snow on the mountains, gleaming like wet sealskin. What a lovely day on the empty road, after the near-miss of the previous night.

Suddenly a small cloud arose near the top of the ridge to my right, then grew as it began silently to descend. I recalled the local people talking about avalanches (*lawine* in German), which I'd never seen but recognized in that soft blob of disturbed white near the top of the slope. I couldn't tell whether the tons of snow would end up on the road ahead of me or behind me (or possibly on top) so it made no sense to run.

I stood still and raised my jacket above my head. It began snowing, got as heavy as a blizzard, and then, at last, lighter again. Soon I was standing under a blue sky. I continued walking for about as long as it had taken to have the cup of coffee and saw the road buried under snow. Again, I suffered no physical harm, but thought for a brief while that I might not escape.

You can't arrange this sort of exposure for a workshop, but it can have benefits. It demonstrates that normal life can suddenly end in accident. But I did not become an aficionado of disaster. I began to live with a consciousness that ordinariness can be interrupted by good outcomes as well as bad (and that we can't always tell which is which).

Much later I heard the Zen story about a monk who was falsely accused of having got a village girl pregnant. "Is that so?" he said, offering to help support and raise the child. Seeing his devotion, the mother was moved, after a while, to confess publicly that the monk was innocent. "Is that so?" he said.

With regard to the incidents in Ischgl, and others like them, I don't know that my response was even a tiny bit enlightened; but those incidents did teach me that things can change suddenly. I had the luxury of learning this lesson without suffering physical harm. But the incidents, including the bike accident in Berkeley, were brisk, intense reminders.

The Transition

Patriarchy has brought us no peace. Instead, its leaders try to reassure us by arguing, as Winston Churchill did, that "safety will be the sturdy child of terror and survival the twin brother of annihilation." What Churchill apparently meant, in his apologia for the nuclear age, was that we could assure survival not by actually annihilating people but by threatening to do so, perpetually, and hoping that no accident or folly would lead to war. Today leaders warn us about terrorists, while themselves commanding the terrible power to wreck, within half an hour, whole continents.

– VICKI NOBLE in *Motherpeace: A Way to the Goddess Through Myth, Art, and Tarot*

ON THE RIGHT SIDE

After divorce, paternal dementia, death of a mentor, and a road accident, I was ready for something completely different. This was the turning point.

One evening I went to a yoga class taught, it turned out, by a Berkeley woman sensitive to gender issues but not closed to male energy. Afterward, she invited me to remain in the studio and paint. I had made no visual images since kindergarten: my mother had saved a crayon drawing of heavy blossoms (one of them in the shape of a yellow six-pointed star), the kind of artifact that only a parent would tuck away. In the yoga teacher's studio we painted with oils on paper. My effort turned into an underwater scene.

I liked painting so much that I went out and bought many tubes of acrylics, plus brushes and hot-pressed acid-free paper. My goal was not to make great art but rather to switch away, at least for a while, from the verbal set to which I'd been largely restricted.

For the next year I made an average of a 24"x 32" painting per week, often working through mealtimes without noticing that I hadn't eaten dinner. I found a book called *Drawing on the Right Side of the Brain*,[1] published by Tarcher (a firm that later put out a pair of my own books). The author was Betty Edwards. Her starting point was the observation from split-brain research that while the language center is on the left side of the brain, some of the crucial skills needed for drawing are on the right.

My challenge in painting was to do something I'd never done except at a childish level thirty-five years or so earlier. Whatever may have qualified me for a good college, it was not an artistic practice. But Edwards argued that most of us have artistic skill, which is blocked by defective "schemata" about how to represent things. Her method starts by by-passing these schemata.

Some aspects of the method are known to any good art teacher, such as focusing on negative space, the space *between* objects. When the edges of negative space are drawn, the objects magically appear, not as you would have drawn them but as you in fact see them.

At the time that I started painting, I had no interest in depicting objects such as we ordinarily see, whether bowls of fruit, faces, landscapes, or mythical scenes. (Nor was I drawn to playing games with the materials of painting.) I wanted to portray something we *don't* see, such as feelings, or ways of thinking, or the play of shapes and colors that didn't necessarily suggest ordinary reality. I regarded painting as a game as strict as tennis.

What were the images "about"? Perhaps some titles will suggest themes. "Finding a Way," "Just After the Beginning," "Fracture Zones," "Dreamtime," "Points of Contact," and "Taking a Line for a Walk." The last of these phrases is borrowed from Paul Klee, whose work helped get me started, especially his magical "Alter Klang."[2] (Please see the color section of this book, on our website, craigkcomstock.com)

Like his colleagues at the Bauhaus, a special school for visual arts, located in Germany, Klee emerged a generation before the New York school of painters. For me, these great European artists of that era bring up a family connection, a missed connection. My mother, frustrated at being told that she could not go to college as her brothers had, suggested to her parents that she might attend the Bauhaus.

Growing up in Milwaukee (which at the time could have been regarded as the furthest west of German cities), the young woman who would become my mother found it natural to train her artistic temperament by attending school in the country of her Berlin ancestors. But her parents did not regard it as proper for a young woman to travel alone to a foreign country. If she had gone, I would not exist, and to venture a less self-centered but equally imponderable question, who knows what art she would have made?

I started painting not to portray what we regard as the real world, but to discover unexplored aspects of myself. I had achieved a little success in the meritocracy of the word, as measured by tests of verbal and mathematical ability and admission to various institutions of higher education. For me, painting was a different realm than anything I had experienced since the age of five.

As a book creation coach and writer, I later returned to the word, though several of my early clients were either creating visual images (a feminist tarot deck) or basing brilliant theories in part on them (ancient Greek pottery). I think the experience of nurturing a part of myself not associated with words made it possible to develop a career as a self-employed professional who placed a high value on curiosity. And I felt a little more whole within myself.

Creative folks often refer to "muses," or they "channel." In any case, the spark feels as if it comes not from them, but from someplace else. As a coach, I never cared where a client felt the spark originated, as long as he or she found it, or as some said, let it come to them.

I don't hang out with celebrities but my boss once invited me to a private dinner with Shirley MacLaine. In a restaurant in Malibu, where everyone was pretending not to notice her, I inquired how she managed to write so many books. "You have other demands, how do you find time?" I asked. "Easy," she replied. "I just take a tape recorder to a cabin I have in the Northwest, and channel the books. I then have the tapes transcribed and touch them up. Do you know anything about channeling?"

It turned out that a client had given me the gift of a weekend workshop on that very phenomenon, part of which was finding one's "guide." From somewhere I found a name, which I repeated to MacLaine. "Your guide and mine are like brother and sister," she said. "Do you want to channel sometime?" My job soon took me away from California, and I could not follow up on this gracious offer.

I mention this story to illustrate the practice of attributing an artistic product to outside sources. Wielding Occam's razor, the instrument meant to produce the simplest explanation, I wonder whether many cultural products come not from an outside being but from a part of the self that is unknown and may feel *as if* it's another being. This seemed a good place to start. Why posit an entity for which there is no evidence?

In the grip of imagining that consciousness is everything, that our species is unconnected to other life-forms, and that this planet is central in the universe, science was held back for centuries until Galileo showed that the earth revolves around the sun, Darwin gave extensive evidence for evolution, and Freud and Jung argued that conscious thought is, so to speak, only a sailboat on the ocean of the unconscious.

As long as we identify wholly with the box of ordinary consciousness we may conclude that any escape from this box involves beings who are located elsewhere. Whether called an unearthly "entity" or a "muse," this creature is assumed to contain more than little us. Any creative act can feel like a gift brought by someone else, if we define ourselves as limited to the being that we know prior to that act. But what if we are more than we know?

A NAME ON THE DOOR

After painting for a while, I began to advance to a kind of liminal space where I was just starting to step over the threshold, where the old had faded away and the new was waiting to appear. On what other guides and practices could I call?

Perhaps this moment is best expressed in a writing from shortly after that period, a brief report on the twenty-fifth anniversary[3] of college graduation. My alma mater invites its graduates at certain anniversaries to tell about their lives and, as a former roommate wrote in the *London Review of*

Books, we spend most of our space on "career achievements and 'exciting' or 'challenging' prospects." I suppose that I did brag about a few small achievements, but I most sought to celebrate a college inspiration that had stayed with me: Here's what I wrote:

> Woody Allen, admirable as a clarinet amateur, has a story about a schlemiel who, through the agency of a magician's box, is transported to visit the literary figure of his choice. Allen's hero chooses Madame Bovary.
>
> For me, the magic of arriving at Harvard led to an even more rusticated eminence. Upon climbing to my assigned room—it was Hollis 31—I found on the door a printed list of previous occupants. Somewhere in the 1830s was the name of Henry David Thoreau.
>
> Having come to college like everyone else to qualify for a profession or other lucrative pastime, I suddenly saw a future centered around a self-made cabin, a bean patch, visions of the Ganges glimpsed in New England waters, and forms of disobedience that were not only civil but literary.
>
> This terrifying self-image was reinforced when John Monro, then dean of the college, honored me with an invitation to assist him, while still an undergraduate, in teaching a course on expository prose, a skill he had watched me learning, in public, gradually, on the *Crimson*. When I asked the dean[4] his model of excellent writing, he suddenly looked even more transcendental and lanky than usual and described a style as compact and polished as an acorn, with noble consequences when it was planted in the mind. I did not have to ask whom he meant.

With this background—reinforced by two of my favorite Harvard authors,[5] F.O. Matthiessen [author of *American Renaissance*] and Stanley Cavell [author of *The Senses of Walden*]—I am not surprised, in looking back at what others call my career, to find a certain tendency to go off to the edge of things (in my case to the Pacific rim), seek to help my society move beyond some of our self-defeating practices, and scribble in books.

The first of these was called *Sanctions for Evil: Sources of Social Destructiveness*, a subject not wholly suitable for the beach or hammock. I have returned to a positive twist on this theme recently in co-editing two books, under the auspices of the Ark Foundation, on the sources of peace and real security [*Citizen Summitry* and *Securing Our Planet*]....

As a quasi-psychologist investigating "adult development," as a consultant to organizations, and now as a foundation executive, [I have followed a] thread through this occupational labyrinth: the idea of social invention—ways to create new forms to keep up with the technological, military, and economic developments that might otherwise overwhelm us.

The grandiosity necessary to this task was nourished in me by the experience, in my [junior] year, of realizing that various small private programs that sent young people abroad to work in the Third World could serve as the model for a similar national effort....

That's the persona that I shared with classmates. A couple of references probably call for more explanation.

On the college paper I wrote a booklet called *Worse Than Futile*,[6] sent around the academic world, and then helped to persuade my own college to turn down funds from the newly passed National Defense Education Act until a McCarthyite "loyalty" oath and affidavit were removed. Many colleges joined the effort, which was led in the Senate by John F. Kennedy.

Through this means, I met the Senator. As an earlier staffer on the *Crimson*, he was happy to help out by writing the Foreword to my report. We then mailed copies to every college president and college newspaper editor in the country. The "loyalty" requirement was soon excised by Congress. It had been unconstitutionally vague and thus open to abuse but, we thought, why wait for the Supreme Court to act rather than spur Congress to fix its own mistake?

Through my brief acquaintanceship with the Senator, I was able to help persuade him of the merits of having the Federal government organize volunteers to work in the third world. All this required was being inspired by some small private programs, and supporting the fairly obvious idea of doing this work on a national scale. The idea, which JFK had the courage to propose in the 1960 Presidential campaign, turned out to be popular and the Peace Corps has endured to the present under both major parties.

When JFK's staff asked me whether U.S. citizens would volunteer to live in third world huts, I said I didn't know but one of the classics of American literature had come from the experiment of dwelling in a simple cabin in the woods near Walden Pond.

CABINS

Henry David Thoreau (or David, as he was then known to friends) is most remembered for being a hermit living in a rustic cabin near a pond, as Martin Luther King Jr. is forever memorialized as the speaker of "I have a dream" on the steps of the Lincoln Memorial. That is how we deal with our prophets, less by suppressing them than by missing their main or more contrarian points and celebrating them for something that's true but a little more acceptable.

King could be praised for non-violence in the service of a positive vision, while his great speech at Riverside Church (exactly a year, to the day, before his assassination) is relatively forgotten. In that speech he talked about poverty, institutional racism, and the Vietnam war, which he said was fought disproportionately *by* people of color against a people *of* color.

Thoreau is quite rightly praised for appreciating nature and describing it closely ("in wildness is the preservation of the world"). But why did he build and sojourn in that cabin[7] near Walden pond? To what extent did he question the heart of U.S. technological striving, acquisitiveness, and empire building? In what ways did he propose other values?

I thought of his cabin when later moving to a ranch in the hills between Stanford and the Pacific. Exploring the ranch, I found the remains of a little shack at the edge of the redwoods, looking across a swath of pasture and a rumple of hills toward the ocean. The unmarried sisters who owned the ranch told me the structure had been built by Thorstein Veblen, author of *The Theory of the Leisure Class*. When I lived on the ranch, only the floor of Veblen's hide-away remained, around which were growing some albino redwood saplings. I don't know why he made this act of inconspicuous consumption at the edge of that forest, but we do know about Thoreau's sylvan thoughts, because he shared some of them in *Walden*.

Was Thoreau a hermit hiding out in the woods? Well, for

a short while he could be portrayed that way, except even then he kept coming into town, which was nearby, and some of the time he invited guests into his cabin and he talked to people on his walks. He wasn't a hermit.

Was he a naturalist? Of course he was. His love and close observation of the natural world is exemplary, but he was more: he was a social critic. He used nature as a contrast to civilized life, which in his view was often boring and, even worse, distracting.

Why did he go to the woodlot of his friend, Mr. Emerson? He tells us quite explicitly. "I went to the woods[8] because I wished to live deliberately…" He wanted to stop relying on unconscious habits. "I went to the woods … to front only the essential facts of life, and see if I could not learn what it [life] had to teach…" (Elsewhere he writes that "in some remote glen in the woods he fronts the elements incased in ice and snow.") Today we might say not "fronts," but confronts. encounters, comes in contact with. Thoreau wanted to wake up and absorb a lesson. Why? He wanted to avoid "when I came to die, discover[ing] that I had not lived."

Thoreau used a soup bone metaphor that is no longer apparent in an age of ready-made meals. "I wanted to live deep and suck all the marrow out of life, to live so sturdily and Spartan-like as to put to rout all that was not life…" He wanted not to eliminate other people from his orbit, but to discover what was basic, not be endlessly distracted.

This was his goal; the cabin, the bean field, the dips in the pond, the walks were means. Thoreau gently ridicules the anxiety of townspeople imagining his situation: was he lonely? Perhaps living in a different way was as startling as being stopped in your tracks by a flower, or cloud, or rippling water, stopped because you actually see them.

Anybody can do it. After I had started meditating at dawn in a little group, I recall seeing a tree that was budding. Ordinarily I would have glanced, thought with a smile "it's spring," and gone on. But I stopped and stared at the tree. I thought if there were no other trees in the world, people would fly thousands of miles to stand before this tree, and feel the wonder of it. Yet, like everything else, it was there all the time. Thoreau could not have described the natural world without having been absorbed, even entranced.

With regard to the human life around him, Thoreau struck discordant notes. Seeing a civilization that took pride in acquiring, he wrote that "a man is rich in proportion to the number of things which he can afford to let alone" and advised his readers to "simplify," a word that he repeated. Wanting to live in a republic rather than an empire, he opposed the war with Mexico. Observing the encroachment of technology, such as the telegraph, he doubted the profundity of messages that would be sent on it. (If he were alive now, we'd perhaps not be able to "follow" him on a social network.) Knowing that classical Athens was much smaller than the metropolitan areas to which we now look for "culture," he thought that a settlement even as small as Concord could produce a great culture, in contrast to its actual provincialism.

It's a wonder that Thoreau didn't end up like Socrates or, to stay closer to home, the "witches" of Salem. He kept doubting what almost everybody else accepted as normal. His big saving grace was his sharing, in words, his attunement to the natural world. When he wasn't scolding people, he was celebrating the world that lay just beyond the settlements, a world in which readers could take pride simply by noticing it, even if they hadn't made nature or sold it or even consumed a bit of it.

What did I mainly take from Thoreau as I set out to build a new life? Not a retreat from people, not even a glorification of nature. I took his praise of simplification and slowness, the appreciation of values other than those thoughtlessly adopted by many, and the steady attention to a reality not consisting solely of things that we fabricate. In the 1980s it was possible to preserve great freedom of action by committing to a simple life.

FLOW

What else did I have to build a new life with?

At Stanford, my program had been about social imagination, wherever it is found. I was especially interested in activities worth doing for their own sakes, not done to get other kinds of rewards. As I found, this overlapped with "flow," the concept propounded by a University of Chicago psychologist named Mihaly Csikszentmihalyi[9] (hereafter MC).

"Flow" as described by MC is the experience of forgetting everything else, including time, because what you're doing is so absorbing (and so demanding) that it requires (and rewards) full attention. Examples include rock climbing, surgery, and jazz. Rock climbing may get you to the top (of Yosemite's Half Dome, for example), surgery may cure a patient (by removing a tumor, say), and jazz may pay off (a lucrative gig or a recording contract); but in the moment these activities are all immediately rewarding as they flow along, an expression of skill and creativity.

Given the vast number of books, it's not often that friends are inspired, separately, by the same one. After many youthful adventures with my brother, we lived far apart and fell out of close contact for several decades, except for occasional flights in his hot air balloon and such family occasions as the death of our father and the marriage of Bruce's daughter. Now we live in the same town and talk regularly over mocha. It turns out that, like me, he was deeply influenced years ago by a book we'd never previously mentioned to each other. It was by MC.

I read *Beyond Boredom and Anxiety* during the period when my life was falling apart and when I had briefly resumed my graduate school research into ludic activity. The concept of flow was a close-to-perfect expression, in psychology, of one aspect of ideas that I'd been developing in the early 1970s under the rubric of "play," especially the play of grownups.

MC's enormous contribution was to focus on absorption in an activity that become its own reward. In other words, if you enter the flow of an activity so thoroughly that you forget yourself and everything else external to that activity, you can experience a kind of bliss. It was MC's genius to look past the difference in skill sets and even the material consequences of various examples of flow, and notice a similar absorption in the moment during certain activities.

What touched my brother in MC's work was the feeling that Bruce had in piloting balloons, especially in the demanding world of competition (which might involve getting to a specified crossroads and dropping a marker, in an aerial device that can't be steered or propelled except by finding the right winds at various altitudes). The challenge of estimating wind speed and direction depended on weather reports, the drift of clouds, the movement of other hot air balloons and of small weather balloons that were sometimes launched, and other clues, including, in Bruce's case, dropped marshmallows. The point is, the challenge of navigating (and of flying safely) was totally absorbing.

In jazz playing, especially to the degree that the music

is improvisatory apart from a basic melodic line, constant alertness, repeated quick response, and musical imagination would take up one's whole attention.

Another early inspiration for me was the Dutch historian Johan Huizinga, author of *Homo Ludens* or "mankind playing." For him, play was not only the activity of children, but also the form in which much of adult culture had evolved.

Our culture in much of the "advanced world" is dominantly about economic success. Clearly, humans need such things as food and water, shelter, a certain temperature range, in most cases a mate, friends, and a measure of security, but beyond that, what are we doing? One answer is piling up more of what is basic, beyond our needs. Another is doing things because they're absorbing. (Some, of course, may be both.)

One example of the latter is music, or in the case of my wife Shoshanah, painting. You normally can't eat the result of what Ellen Dissanayake calls "artifying," or defeat enemies with it. If you lack the basics, as hundreds of millions do, the deprivation hurts. But if we have the basics and lack imagination about what *else* to do, we may also suffer.

These ruminations are not original. One American experiment, as we have seen, was conducted by Thoreau. His famous sojourn at Walden pond, as he tried to point out, was less about solitude than about the discovery of what was worth doing after securing the basics of a life that, in Duane Elgin's phrase, is outwardly simple, inwardly rich.

Recent research suggests that, for work at the high end of the creativity scale, more "compensation" may actually *reduce* output; in that case, motivators are not only money, but also such factors as autonomy, community, and purpose. To the extent this finding is validated, it would call for a big adjustment in the field of economics. This would be an inconvenient truth, because while money is easy to measure, those other values are not.

In play, certain moves can be expected, but others are a surprise. Creativity favors those who can accept surprises, perhaps even welcome them.

On an early date, my future wife and I decided to collaborate on a painting. This was a challenge for me, because she was, in her spare time, a devoted painter and had been since childhood, while I was an amateur at best. The rules were simple. One person would take a turn with the brushes, and then give the paper to the other. You were meant to engage with what the other person had done, not go off to a private corner of the paper.

You could embroider the other's gesture, put it in a new context, introduce another theme, reinforce what the first person had done, or make an ironic (visual) comment. What you couldn't do was paint over the other person's work, in the sense of concealing it. When the paper was full, about ten turns each, we stopped.

This exercise was a way of having a conversation without speaking words. Part of the fun was almost forgetting who had done what. We were rivals in being interesting, collaborators in making something wonderful. Most of all, we were playing together.

A CLIENT

I still had no occupation to replace my earlier plan to become a professor (and consultant). A fascination with play doesn't buy groceries or pay the rent. My new career began as a surprise to me when a friend asked for help in writing a twenty-four-page booklet that would briefly explain each of the Tarot cards in the deck that she had just designed with a collaborator. This brief manual would fit in the box with the deck of cards, which were round and had the name of "Motherpeace." The friend was Vicki Noble.[10]

It quickly became clear to me that she had a depth of wisdom that could lead to a series of full-length books. By the end of the lunch, my friend had decided to write her first book, which has been in print ever since.

Through this work, I became a book creation coach. I wasn't a ghostwriter or "told to" guy, though these are honorable professions. Instead, I set out to coach authors who wanted to write their own books but who felt they could benefit from having someone to ask questions, help in arranging research and schedules, and offer comments.

Although most of my professional relationships were confidential, a little like those of an attorney or psychotherapist, some authors chose to acknowledge in print our work together. Vicki Noble was one.

Inherently interdisciplinary, Vicki was a brilliant intuitive researcher, an engaging writer. (I use the past tense to refer to our work in the early 1980s.) A feminist, she was nonetheless open to working with a man. Responsive to challenge and suggestion, she didn't always agree with me, but always entered into dialogue and thus was fun to work with.

When we first talked over lunch, she wanted help with writing, and I wanted to find out a little about Tarot. It was then that I first heard about the "fool" card.[11] Until meeting Vicki, I'd used "fool" mainly as an epithet, but she explained that, in Tarot, this archetype is neither an idiot nor a Shakespearean fool, a character who is licensed to tell the truth in humor to a ruler.

Instead of necessarily speaking truth to power, the Tarot Fool is a character who steps off the edge into the unknown, who starts things. At lunch, Vicki said that, in this sense,

I was a fool, a person with beginner's mind. I knew it was the start of an almost perfect friendship.

Vicki's judgment of my character had immediate resonance for me because when I had visited Japan, where my sister Kani was director of a language school, she decided to order for me the gift of a *hanko*, a personal seal carved in horn which, pressed to an ink pad, is used as a sort of signature. But what characters to use? In Japanese, my first name and middle initial are pronounced ka-rei-gu-kou. In Japanese aesthetics, "karei" can mean something like "magnificent." "Gukou" is "folly." Allowing for the ambivalence of sibling-speech, I heard not foolishness, but the style of a beginner.

Cover of Motherpeace by Vicki Noble

My sister's gift and the lunch with Vicki are the origins of this book, which is about starting things for which I had no formal qualifications or, in at least one case, no intention. Stepping into the unknown does not always work out well, but fear keeps us from starting many experiences that *could* succeed. I guess one of the skills for an explorer, as for a poker player, is knowing when to cut losses and get out, and when to double down and go further.

When the U.S. bought the territory now comprising the state of Alaska, it was known as "Seward's Folly," but no one is laughing about the purchase now. William Seward was Secretary of State under Andrew Johnson, and I suppose he had the precedent, sixty-four years earlier, of Thomas Jefferson's equally foolish decision to make the Louisiana Purchase. Without comparing myself to these risk-taking statesmen, I admire their style.

At the meeting with Vicki, tarot interested me more as a system of characterology than as a predictive method. Another example of the former is the Enneagram,[12] a nine-point system for describing types of personality fixations. All of the points are limiting. The goal is to evolve.

In this evolution it's useful to keep asking Montaigne's question, "what do I know?" I once claimed, rather grandiosely, that I could quickly make a list of hundreds of things I *didn't* know. It was in the 1980s that I realized that a much longer list could be made, but not by me, of things I don't even know exist. This account is about a slight shortening of the later list.

I'm told that Buddhists have a phrase, "beginner's mind,"[13] which refers to an ability to start afresh. I take pride in knowing, but when this pride gets set aside, I sometimes move a little closer to what is called "source matrix," the bubbling soup pot out of which almost anything can take shape.

One way to restore humility is to offer to help people who know enough about a subject to write a book about it. At first I would make use of my ignorance by asking clients to explain their subject. This was not a waste of effort for them. Most clients were looking for an audience larger than other specialists. At some point, however, I would realize it was necessary to acquire a closer feel for their area. It was this need that lured me into worlds about which I hadn't known. I would receive expert instruction, which often took the form of "workshops" or other direct experience.

With Vicki, for example, I was drawn into a world of feminist history and archetypal speculation. While my ignorance helped assure clients that I could not become a rival, my curiosity made me a natural student, and my personal background and approach generated questions that in some cases were new to clients (but would occur to many readers).

Because not enough good people were offering the services of a book creation coach, at least in the San Francisco Bay Area, I had more prospective clients than I could accept and thus, like a college with a good reputation, I could be selective. My main criteria for clients were willingness to respond to suggestions (which did not necessarily mean agreement) and potential to nudge the culture in what I thought was a good direction.

Although I call Vicki my first client, as a grad student I had performed editorial tasks for professors, including Nevitt Sanford, for whom I later edited a collection of his papers on higher education (*Learning After College*). I suppose that helping authors was a natural use of talents that had been called forth by college journalism. However, work for a fee with a non-academic author did not begin until 1982.

COACHING AUTHORS

My clients generally wanted to reach an audience of non-specialists, whether the subject was, for example, gender issues, art, nutrition, ancient history, modern politics, sociability, aging well, or many others.

With a little help, a client could not only enjoy the process of writing a book but also meet deadlines. When Vicki's book was finished on time, the publisher hardly knew what to do with the submission, accustomed to piteous appeals for extensions of the contractual date for completion. Among certain publishers I was developing a reputation as someone who helped clients get projects done on time, in good condition. This was largely a tribute to my clients, who did the writing.

It is relevant to my topic of going out of my comfort zone to tell about one early project that I took on a dare. The manuscript was already completed and had even been sent to a dozen publishers by a capable New York agent. None of the publishers had offered a contract. What was to be done?

The author flew out to the San Francisco Bay Area and we talked for a week, mainly prompted by my questions. I suggested that she write a new first and last chapter, the first posing a mystery well known to scholars, and the last offering a solution that her research revealed. These chapters would be discursive rather than, like the rest of the book, analytical history.

The new manuscript was accepted by a major New York publishing house within a fortnight of being submitted. This was fun. (And when the commercial run was over, the book was picked up by a major university publisher.)

Academic authors made up just a small fraction of my client list, which was composed mainly of workshop leaders, political activists, psychotherapists, and people in other non-academic professions. The academics often wanted to reach an audience beyond their own fields, but felt it would be demeaning to "popularize." I would tell them that writing in standard English for non-specialists called for great clarity and consideration of the implications of special knowledge and, at its best, was at least as challenging as academic prose.

This work as a book creation coach put me in touch with

some of the most profound and engaging thinkers of our time. Each had quirks, as did I. My attitude was that as long as someone is doing socially useful work, personal quirks are easy to excuse or simply overlook. I loved the way clients were willing to struggle to shape their experience and insights in ways useful to readers.

It was clients who led or pushed me into worlds that they knew but that were unfamiliar to me. After my higher education, I knew a little about politics, literature, and "personality theory," but beyond that lay vast areas of unknowing.

Having a brush with journalism while reporting for my college paper and, briefly, for a newsmagazine, I unconsciously sought a career that would allow me to function as a "social neutrino." I heard this phrase from a Russian sociologist in Moscow. He was describing a colleague "who, like a neutrino, could pass easily through walls."

Many careers isolate a person with others of their kind, or at least others in the same organization. One reason that detectives are so popular as the leading characters in TV shows is that the crimes they investigate take them into many different social settings. Of course we like to find out "who done it" and we like to have order restored, but meanwhile we like to be led into other worlds. (In the case of TV or the movies we are taken there without peril or even the need to visualize.)

I wish I could say that I moved easily and effortlessly into new worlds, but my first reaction was sometimes skeptical. I was doubtful, uncomfortable. I wanted to go there to help my clients, but I often didn't think the new world would welcome me, or that it had a message for me personally. Again and again, I was wrong.

I want to illustrate this process with a few detailed examples. One example concerns sex and relationships; a second, the patterns that I'd adopted from my parents; a third, an unexpected and unusual kind of experience; and a fourth, what seemed like an impossible political challenge.

ART BY AUTHOR

In addition to *Washi Arcs*, reproduced on the section pages of this book, digital color illustrations of paintings by the author are available online, without charge, at craigkcomstock.com. (In the Kindle version, click on the thumbnails below.)

1. *From the Source* (also reproduced on a ceramic mug given to subscribers by public radio)

2. *Lake District* (the one in the mountains in the north of Italy)

3. *Shield for Angie* (made for a year-long workshop led by Angeles Arrien and held in Sausalito, California)

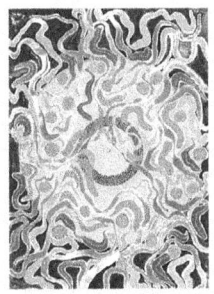 4. *Ten Thousand Things* (a Buddhist commonplace)

 5. *Almost Blue* (part of a series featuring a neon-bright crescent moon)

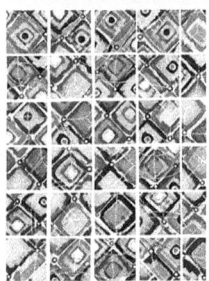 6. *Dreamtime* (a word purloined from the Australian aborigines)

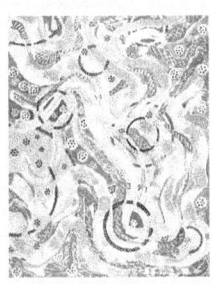 7. *Finding a Way* (could almost be called "Enlarging a Comfort Zone")

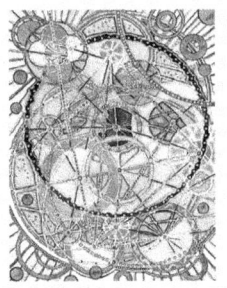 8. *Just After the Beginning* (the big circle is an allusion to the concept of "beginner's mind")

Some Adventures

3

A Tantric Initiation

Most [people] either have had peak experiences through sex or feel intuitively that they are achievable. Because we know that such moments are possible, each time we enter into lovemaking, we secretly hope that this time we will enjoy them again. We hold the vision of a deeply fulfilling and joyful embrace, in which the vibrant pleasure of the body encompasses the delight of the heart, the meeting of minds, and the mutual recognition of kindred spirits.

– MARGO ANAND, *The Art of Sexual Ecstasy*

Friends of a friend had invited me to lunch on their large wooden dock at the north end of Lake Tahoe: a plate of smoked salmon on the tablecloth, the buzz of water skiing in the distance, sunlight on ripples. A couple of guests arrived a little late and walked down a long sloping ramp to the dock. One was a striking woman who sized up the situation and sat opposite the one man who wasn't either married or gay. It happened to be me. Some flirting occurred.

A friend had told me that Margo Anand[1] had written a book in her native French on ecstasy; was known, in Europe and beyond, as "the tantra queen"; and led workshops. I wish I could say that I was not just a bit flattered by the attentions of a woman known as a teacher of sexual liberation. Why me? Perhaps I made her laugh.

I had several reasons to keep Margo at a distance. She had just come from "the ranch," an Oregon facility created by followers of Bhagwan Shree Rajneesh,[2] a guru who was later known as Osho and who had attracted many American and European disciples to his ashram not far from the city that we now call Mumbai. Rajneesh was a prolific author, an incessant giver of spiritual talks in meetings known as "darshan," and leader of a global movement. It turned out that Margo, while happy to get away from the intrigues of the Oregon ranch, had been a star teacher in the Rajneesh ashram in India.

I am allergic to gurus, almost as some people get hay fever from pollen, but since a childhood viewing of the 1953 film about Martin Luther, I have been fascinated by the phenomenon of religious leaders. Not to compare the two, but here was a contemporary, rather than someone from the 16th century. And he had chosen a person at our lunch table as a teacher at his ashram. Why? Margo was author of a French book, the title of which could be translated as *The Path to Ecstasy*. And she had the background to teach tantra, a spiritual path much favored by Rajneesh.

But an Eastern guru was not for me. I'd never been closer to India than Greece far to the west, and Japan, far to the northeast. I did not like "movements," which kept reminding me, unfairly I'm sure, of the Germans of the 1930s and early 1940s mobilizing behind an absolute leader who took total responsibility.

However, tantra intrigued me. It was an inversion of the Puritanical avoidances, or at least prohibitions, of Dad's ancestors in colonial New England. As I learned from Margo, the basic idea was not to deny or struggle against natural impulses, but to devote them consciously to the cause of spiritual advancement. Thus sex, and other occasions of ecstasy, could, she said, be doorways to the divine.

INVERNESS

Before long, Margo and I were arranging to rent a house together on Point Reyes peninsula. This is a semi-wild area north of San Francisco, adjacent to the Golden Gate National Recreation Area. Geologically, the peninsula rests on a tectonic plate separate from the one that includes the rest of California and beyond it all the rest of the forth-eight contiguous states. In geological time the peninsula has migrated north from at least as far as the coast of what is now Los Angeles and will end up, scientists tell us, in Alaska. Surrounded by beaches, Point Reyes centers on a mountain called Vision, and in the middle has a trail through woods over a hill to the ocean. Running on this trail in morning fog, I once saw a herd of albino deer leaping along, through winter birches, parallel to the trail. I felt they were almost companions in that pale world.

The town of Point Reyes was small but promising and unusual. In the mid 1980s, an art gallery there had a show of Soviet paintings. The restaurant served a great bowl of stew made with oysters grown and shucked locally. The bookshop was obviously independent; the school, the kind where many outlying students arrive from rural houses by bus. Quaint B&Bs could be found in their own groves. The smell of cow dung wafting over the short main street said to me, "you're almost home."

Margo had a contract to write a book in English. I was becoming known as a coach who worked with authors. It was a match made in heaven, though we agreed that any work together on her book on sexuality was secondary to our being together. As she said, we'd "practice," and she'd write. I was meanwhile working on a pair of books for the Ark Foundation, published as *Citizen Summitry: Keeping the Peace When It Matters Too Much to Be Left to Politicians* and as *Securing Our Planet: How to Succeed When Threats are Too Risky and There's Really No Defense* (Tarcher, 1986).

Margo and I moved into a house overlooking the slim bay, which was almost like a section of a wide river, across which we could see ranches on the mainland. When not writing, Margo led workshops, and so was accustomed to talking in front of rooms full of people who had paid to learn the secrets of better sex and relationships. In Inverness, we were almost alone, as neighbors left each other largely to themselves. I would talk with other bike riders I met, people running on the several nearby beaches, hiking a trail up the mountain, gathering oysters, or loading big cans of milk. On the phone and on weekly trips to the UC Berkeley library, I'd find other writers who were envisioning a world beyond the Cold War.

I was a little anxious about isolating ourselves, but Margo said otherwise she wouldn't write, and after the intensity of occasional workshops she wanted to get away from circles of eager students. So we had each other, which for me was a delight. On each day of the week I rode to a different beach on which to run, biking among the dairy farms. We had visitors from Europe, on their way to the glories of San Francisco or Hawaii or lands further west. Margo's publisher came by, and later became mine.

She and I went away from Inverness mainly to meet her workshop schedule and to interview people for her book, including a scholar of yoga and the staff at a sexual enhancement school in the East Bay. During the free Friday night events before her paid weekend workshops, I would sit with her on a bench as she explained what she'd teach.

A TANTRIC INITIATION

Workshops were held at a hot spring, in a motivational speaker's house in southern California, and the next summer at a big old farmhouse in the north of Switzerland and a "zentrum" in Berlin. It was a world I hadn't known. It took me a while to realize I was looked on with awe or at least curiosity as the partner of the teacher.

Once a week or so, I'd go "over the hill" from our home near Inverness to the more inhabited parts of the Bay Area, through eastern Marin, all the way to Emeryville, which adjoined Berkeley and which was the site of my client Don Carlson's office in a tall building bearing his company's name. From his window we could see San Francisco and the Golden Gate bridge.

To some of Margo's students, tantra might have meant something like sexual enhancement. To my brother-in-law, who had studied Tibetan Buddhism, or to my friend Stuart Sovatsky, a long-time yogi, tantra was a secret doctrine associated with south Asian religions. I admired Margo for teaching what she taught and for giving Rajneesh credit even when he became, in some circles, a tad suspect.

Based on videos, I regarded Rajneesh as an enormously talented explainer and a bit of a rascal, whatever else he was. He was given to raiding various spiritual traditions (eventually, he wrote a "Bible"). To him, tantra meant not struggling against urges of the body (as celibate priests or monks try to do) but transforming them into occasions for spiritual growth.

So I found myself being the partner of an international teacher of sexual enhancement. Although I may have helped her a little in getting started on her book, we related primarily in ways other than coach and client. However, her book project was always there. While visiting in the south of France she called me in California and complained that the burden of completing a big book was making "a nun" of her, which she observed was ironic considering her subject. On bad days, she was almost tempted to give back the advance and abandon the project.

I had several people to see in Europe and said I'd visit her and try to help. We met in an old farmhouse in Provence. She'd written out on cards each point she wanted to develop, each scene she intended to describe, each stage to explore. In a day we laid out the cards on a big stone floor, and kept rearranging, until she felt the sequence worked. Then we simply picked up the hundreds of cards in order and fastened them with rubber bands. Each day thereafter she would just take the top card and convert it into prose. Steadily, the book took shape. Voila!

SEXUAL LIBERATION

Tantra, in Margo's sense, was a definite step in the sexual liberation of the West. Way back in 1972 Alex Comfort had published *The Joy of Sex*, and the next year *More Joy of Sex*. His main point is that most sex is fun and skillful sex, even better, as good food is delicious: the first book even bore the subtitle *A Gourmet Guide to Lovemaking*. His approach was liberatory but not primarily "spiritual." What Margo's book added was an approach to sex that, while physically explicit, could lead to an exalted state of consciousness.

Tantric sex got the reputation, in the West, of being slow, a forerunner of the movements for slow food and slow money. But it was not so much slow as ritualized and approached as more than, to quote a French wit, the friction of two skins. In Hindu tantra, the man is seen as a representation of the god Shiva; the woman, of the goddess Shakti. Sex is thus an enactment that is less personal than, as Margo put it, profound.

Seeing a sexual partner as a sacred being made lovemaking less like Alex Comfort's gourmet meal than like a celebration. Both were ways out of the Puritan closet, but despite overlaps, quite different. The one led to enjoyment for its own sake (*jouissance* in the French); the other, to a heightened focus and sense of occasion. Comfort helped set the tone of the 1970s; Margo, of a consciousness that came into its own in the 1980s and remains alive, in some circles, today.

Because of the Hollywood "code" governing depiction of lovemaking, nearly all movies show lovers approaching one another frantically, as if they were in a frenzy. To be "hot" is to be passionate, which means intense and fast. Clothes are almost ripped off. (In fact, a genre of novels has been called the "bodice ripper.") It is ironic that any teenager equipped with a smart phone can access the distortions of pornography, but when he or she enters a movie theater is almost always shown only an explosive onset, usually but not always followed perhaps by the lovers talking in bed, sometimes still over cigarettes.

In contrast to this half-seen model of explosiveness, tantra's reputation for slowness means that, alas, it must take too long for busy lives. Margo explained tantra is about forgetting any goal and staying as intensely as possible in the moment, playing like a child in a sphere not yet available, in adult form, to children. Is sex about reproduction? Sometimes, yes. But it can also, Margo taught, be about "relaxing into a higher and higher state of arousal."

This sounds paradoxical. We're taught to think of arousal as frantic, not as relaxed. The two concepts don't seem to go together.

Pornography is generally about a man getting off and a woman pretending meanwhile to enjoy, for example, photogenic spurts on their face or breasts. The rest can't as easily be shown. In a largely visual culture, this is the sexual instruction most widely available.

Marching from one goal to the next, many lovers, Margo said, may miss everything else. Tantra is about everything else, too. The point is not to take a lot of time. It's quite possible to be mentally absent for long periods of time. The point is to be present, in which case not rushing is natural.

Margo often told her workshops that male orgasm lasts ten seconds (give or take), in which case if a youngish guy has one every other day, or 183/year, that adds up to 1,830 seconds, or about a half hour per year (this is only an approximation, she said, but do the math). For this duration of pleasurable paroxysm, researchers tell us, we think about sex every few minutes in the case of men or a little less often in the case of the average woman.

Margo was not against orgasm, quite the contrary, but what she was *for* is consciousness all during sex, not a sort of race to the finish line. Presence is one feature of tantra; a dwelling in the state of arousal. Another? Using sexual energy not as an escape *from* life, but as energy *for* life. Clearly, tantra is anti-Puritan, and Margo, as a French woman, saw many other cultures as Puritan despite a glaze of sexuality used to sell products.

It's typical of a practice being brought from one culture to another, that the receiving culture may seek to "domesticate" the practice, to bring it within familiar categories. Thus, tantra can seem a kind of sexual enhancement on the familiar model. For example, tantra teaches seeing the partner as if he or she were a divine being. This can seem ridiculous to a harried couple focused on dealing with the challenges of the day, putting the kids to bed, getting enough sleep to function in a busy tomorrow. In this scenario, the partners may see each other less as divine than as mistake-making, non-caring, defective, all-too-human.

Margo regarded tantra as a way of being in the world that is a challenge to our consumer culture. That culture is dedicated to keeping busy, to making contacts, to showing results, to demonstrating that we have merit. Again, nothing wrong with these activities, but, she would ask, what is the true cost? As markets are distorted by hidden "externalities," so life is made thin by having always to rush. You can see why her approach appealed to me, drawn as I was to "play," and to getting outside routine and comfort zones.

However, having been raised with the model of partners for life, a model exemplified by my parents, I was unfamiliar with the concept of making love in the same period with many partners, each one of whom was treated as an embodiment of a divinity. It was clear that Margo was sincere in her version of polyamory, which was also exemplified by some in my social circles who did not invoke "tantra."

I'm grateful for the time that I spent with, and all that I learned from, Margo, especially about ecstasy and about awareness, a lesson not extended until much later when, in a different key, I worked with a meditation teacher. I still hear Margo's laughter.

4

A Glorious Surprise

One conclusion was forced upon my mind at that time, and my impression of its truth has ever since remained unshaken. It is that our normal waking consciousness, rational consciousness as we call it, is but one special type of consciousness, whilst all about it, parted from it by the filmiest of screens, there lie potential forms of consciousness entirely different. We may go through life without suspecting their existence; but apply the requisite stimulus, and at a touch they are there in all their completeness, definite types of mentality which probably somewhere have their field of application and adaptation. No account of the universe in its totality can be final which leaves these other forms of consciousness quite disregarded.

– WILLIAM JAMES, *The Varieties of Religious Experience*

There are experiences that most of us are hesitant to speak about, because they do not conform to everyday reality and defy rational explanation. These are not particular external occurrences, but rather events of our inner lives, which are generally dismissed as figments of the imagination and barred from our memory. Suddenly the familiar view of our surroundings is transformed in a strange, delightful, or alarming way: it appears to us in a new light, takes on a special meaning. Such an experience can be as light and fleeting as a breath of air, or it can imprint itself deeply upon our minds.

– ALBERT HOFMANN, *LSD My Problem Child: Reflections on Sacred Drugs, Mysticism, and Science*

Around the time of meeting Margo, I had an experience that was unsought, as well as astonishing. It arose not in the context of relationships, family life, or world affairs. It came as a surprise, felt like an enormous gift, and taught me that I didn't know and couldn't even guess at all that life had to offer.

Uninfluenced by any experience with psychedelic molecules, whether synthesized by Dr. Hofmann or supplied by a psychiatrist or shaman, I was surprised at the age of forty-three by an experience of distinct, spontaneous, and prolonged bliss. In Hofmann's words, my world was transformed in a strange and delightful way, an experience imprinted deeply on my mind. Having overcome my hesitancy to speak, I want to share what I know of this surprise, while resisting the temptation to impose any single "rational explanation." What James calls "the filmiest of screens" can seem like a solid wall until it blows aside. Here is one experience of what lies beyond.

GURUS

In the early 1980s some of my friends in the Bay Area were responding to gurus, both imported and domestic. By guru, I mean a spiritual teacher in the Eastern tradition of obedience and practice followed by students in the hope of enlightenment. I was skeptical about spiritual leaders, in part because I'd grown up in a church and left it, in part because of a stubborn urge to "do it myself," and in part because of *Triumph of the Will,* by Leni Riefenstahl, a documentary films about the rise of Hitler.

Of course her film was in a political context, not spiritual. It showed devotion to Nazism, blind devotion to a leader who would take all responsibility, who told how it was, and who demanded absolute obedience. I saw the vast and obvious distinction between Adolf Hitler and Ramana Maharshi, but preferred a skeptical style of learning.

With regard to spiritual matters, I was curious but full of questions. In the Bay Area I attended a number of satsangs with gurus, read various books, and talked on many occasions with someone closely involved with Da Free John[1] (as he was then known). I thought Da was worth investigating, in part because he'd written a fetching spiritual autobiography called *The Knee of Listening*, and in part because he was praised by the master of "integral" development, Ken Wilbur.

What I was told in the form of inside gossip was that Da seemed to have reservations about the "mediocre" lives of his followers and seemed to be teaching them how to fly a stunt plane when, in his view, some of them couldn't even hobble across the tarmac and climb into the pilot's seat.

I had various other contacts with Eastern religions, including a brother-in-law[2] who was drawn to Tibetan Buddhism to the point of learning the language and spending time in Nepal on a Fulbright, time that included the directing of a feature-length film, *Lord of the Dance/ Destroyer of Illusion*. In Manhattan in the mid 1970s I had arranged a supper club with him: each week we would meet at a certain Chinese restaurant where the menu was wholly in ideograms, unfamiliar to both of us, and where we would chat over feasts that included bitter melon, hot peppers, and unfamiliar parts of pigs.

Back in the San Francisco Bay Area, I also had an opportunity to interview Ram Das, who was careful to call himself a teacher not a guru. When I teased him about the distinction, saying that his insisting on it probably caused followers to trust him even more deeply, he just smiled seraphically.

What I'm suggesting, by these examples, was that enlightenment and spiritual experience were in the air in the 1980s. People would disappear to an ashram in India, an island in the south Pacific, yoga retreats in Hawaii or Mexico, or evenings in Marin County at the local Buddhist facility called Spirit Rock, led by Jack Kornfield. The range of styles was wide.

What I mainly did was talk with followers, and read books. I never went to a retreat, or even took instruction in meditation. Which made the experience I call "Koya" all the more unexpected, not to say totally undeserved.

In an article in the *New York Review of Books,* I recently saw the Bay Area described as an "alternate reality," and like Manhattan, it is. The world of San Francisco contained much that was not only unusual, but also in some respects silly. It also offered much that was valuable and pioneering.

Most people think the area they have chosen is especially blessed. Apart from a few years each in New England, in Europe, and in Manhattan, I lived all of my pre-retirement adult life in the San Francisco Bay Area. Though born in the Midwest I know little about it, or the South or, apart from many vacation visits, the Southwest. Unlike my Dad, whose work took him to all fifty states, I have explored mainly within the diverse social and cultural circles of one locale.

In the 1980s the San Francisco Bay Area was rich in its welcome to experiences called "spiritual," "psychic," and "mystical." While I knew a little about mystics in the Christian tradition, I had a "show me" attitude toward claims of access to some other realm. I felt the normal realm had more than enough mysteries of its own. Science had made basic discoveries confirmed by naturalistic experiments. I felt that it would be best just to describe any phenomenon that was out of the ordinary, not automatically to regard it as evidence of a supernatural reality.

KOYA

Apart from experiencing the joy of painting and of finding the start of a paying trade, one of the first adventures of my forties happened in the dark, inspired, in part, by an early client's attunement to experience that she called spiritual.

It began late one afternoon in 1983 in Albany, California, when I got tired of writing and editing, went out for an ice cream cone and, while still licking it, saw a poster for a movie called *Koyaanisqatsi*.[3] I not only didn't know what the word meant, but also wasn't even sure how to pronounce it or from what language it came. Koya-anis-kaht-si: a strange name for a movie.

The poster was quite uninviting, consisting, as I recall, only of text. None of the names was familiar. But I'd finished the cone, didn't want to go back to the computer, and wholly as a diversion, bought a ticket and went into the theater.

The movie turned out to have no dialogue, no characters, and no plot in the usual sense. It's big on rockets taking off in slow mo, theatrical southwestern landscapes, rivers meandering through rock layers, fog rolling over hills, cars coursing down freeways, and later defunct public housing projects being demolished. After the first fifteen minutes I almost left. Perhaps I had expected an exotic comedy.

But I stayed and began to enjoy the montage of nature and of cities portrayed as machines. My father, commuting through Grand Central in Manhattan, had complained of feeling like a sheep being herded through gates. (*Koyaanisqatsi* actually includes a scene in that terminal.) As the screen said at the end, the title refers, in the Hopi language, to "a life out of balance; a life that must be changed." I recalled reading something similar in Rilke's poem about the archaic torso of Apollo: *Du muss dein Leben aendern:* you must change your life.

Okay, big talk. At first, I regarded the movie, with a brilliant soundtrack by the composer Philip Glass, as nothing more than an interesting experiment. But in conversing on the phone with a client and friend, I must have made it sound intriguing because she asked whether I'd go again and take her and her partner. I would, hoping to hear their responses and to go a little deeper into a very unusual movie.

In the first ten minutes or so, I felt the anxiety that comes of recommending an experience and later doubting that your friends will like it. Then something began to happen. At first I felt a tingling in my left big toe and soon in both my feet. Half-aware, I wondered if the way I was sitting had cut off the circulation in my legs, but the tingling was different, not at all uncomfortable, more like the space of my feet and legs being filled with thin warm honey. As I watched the movie, this pleasant feeling began to rise in my legs, then higher in my body. When it reached my shoulders, this sensation of flow seemed to go simultaneously down my arms and up through my head.

Then the intensity was turned up, the way you'd increase the volume on an amplifier. I asked my friend to hold my hand, saying that something wonderful was happening, about which I would tell her later, but meanwhile I would appreciate her support. Soon I felt as if a river of light were flowing upward through my body, out the top of my head. I knew that nobody else could see what was happening, but I even felt as if light were also coming out the ends of my fingers. The general effect was ecstatic, more than I'd ever experienced doing anything.

This feeling lasted for the remainder of the movie. When the theater lights were turned on, I got up slowly and found I could walk normally. The boyfriend had to leave, but I invited the woman to stop by my nearby house for five minutes because I wanted to describe what had happened. As I lay down on the living room floor she said brightly, "Since I can type fast, why don't I just turn on your computer and keyboard what you say?" She did. Without being aware of time, I talked for an hour. The next morning I found the whole description had been preserved.

Drawing of Philip Glass, © Chuck Close, courtesy Pace Gallery

The inner experience had not blotted out the movie, but intensified my experience of it. I had been aware of a sharp contrast between the somber, even desperate scenes of urban life and the ecstasy that I was feeling. Why did this feeling begin and build? Was the music a trigger? Was I joyful that somebody else, the director, saw what I'd half-observed? Was it the immense power of images with no words?

The quotations that follow are from the typing done by my friend as I lay on the floor trying to tell her about what had happened in the theater. My words were calm but consisted of ecstatic speech, as I attempted to describe a world that I'd never imagined existing, much less a world that I could enter. In normal reality, I'd almost be embarrassed by some of the language if it weren't the best account of an astonishing experience that I could cobble together. One of the best gifts I have ever been given was the transcript, on my computer, of my account spoken to a friend right after the experience.

Returning from the theater, I began by saying "I am still feeling the same white-water river of energy. It enters through my feet and flows up through my entire body and out my hands and the top of my head." Ordinarily, I resisted talk about "energy" in the body, but I couldn't think of a more apt description.

I felt as if I were channeling a flow of light. "In fact, the visual image that best describes this energy was the rapid movement of cars on a night-time freeway where, as in *Koyaanisqatsi*, one sees bands of headlights moving around corners and over slight hills, never stopping." What would ordinarily look like rush hour seemed like an inexorable and lovely dance.

"I felt the light come in through the ground and move through me and go out toward the images on the screen and toward the people who appeared there." Some of the images were of mechanical life in big cities, the scuttle of grim people on sidewalks, the wasteland of abandoned housing projects. "Every time I would see a person who looked lost, lonely or fearful, I felt this flow of light going directly toward them and heard a voice saying, 'yes, this is for you, too.'"

While I was describing the experience, it began to grow stronger. "It is a cool fire. Although I am experiencing this for only part of a single evening, I feel it could go on without consuming me. I feel like the bush that was burning and every leaf on the bush remained green and vibrant and the tenderest buds were never singed, but began to open in the midst of the flames."

As if the allusion to Moses weren't enough, the transcript contains several other grandiose analogies. "I feel like the fiery clouds in a Tibetan tanka that roil the sky above Shambhala." As my brother-in-law had taught me, a tanka is a Tibetan painting showing a Buddhist deity or a schematic depiction of the universe; Shambhala, a mythical kingdom in the Himalayas, a kind of "pure land" or paradise.

"I feel like the sky in a painting by a nun in the Middle Ages, where the stars look as big as our sun and send a light that set her soul ablaze. And I feel that for this woman, whose name was Hildegaard von Bingen, her paintings may have been the only way she could try to share with others, within her Christian world, the intensity of what she had seen …. I also think of the so-called crazy monks in Chinese and Japanese ink-brush paintings, who wandered with their begging bowls on paths leading up to (what one of them called) Cold Mountain. Up there, in the midst of fog, they too would see the light and later would descend again when they needed rice and perhaps the chance to see another human face."

This burst of cultural references was perhaps a sign that I had nearly exhausted my description of what happened during the movie.

Perhaps I should add that after this evening, for over six months, all I had to do to let the flow resume was take a couple of deep breaths. During this period I continued to do my professional work, meet with friends, write, and conduct all the normal tasks of life, including some delicate negotiations.

The crucial moment in the movie theater, as I realized

later, came when I felt a tiny signal that would have been easy to turn away from. It was breath stopping to think that I, and probably many others, had felt similar stirrings and ignored them, whereupon I'm sure they simply went away. I also suspected that some other people had let the stirrings build, but then hesitated ever to describe the experience, for fear of being thought unusual.

EARLY ENERGY

Looking back it's possible to identify (or imagine) early signs or hints of a condition that later became manifest and intense. This was true of my father's Alzheimer's, and also of my own experience of bliss. For an example of the latter, when I was a child my mother often got headaches which was probably related to the stress of raising four rather active kids. On a kitchen shelf she kept a big jar of aspirin. At the same time I, with little to worry about, would occasionally get mild headaches, which I cured almost immediately, without stopping to think how.

I'd close my eyes, feel a soft jolt of energy rising from the base of my spine, ascending, and then (as it were) rinsing the inside of my skull. At that point, the headache would vanish. I don't know how I regarded the contrast with my Mom's jumbo supply of acetylsalicylic acid. Perhaps I thought that pills were for grownups with too much to do, or people with a predisposition to headaches. My method of dissolving a headache seemed an ordinary act, as casual as drinking water or taking a nap.

I didn't formally meditate until a decade *after* the period covered by this memoir, but you couldn't live in the Bay Area in the 1960-90s without at least hearing about sitting quietly and becoming aware of breathing. And if like me you had a client who "did energy healing," you heard about "laying on of hands." I don't know of any scientific way to measure what, if anything, is happening in the case of "energy"; but I do know that the lack of a scientific measurement is no proof that a phenomenon doesn't exist.

Thus, when the feeling of flow began in the movie theater, I had the background of modest flashes, at least, of something like "energy," as well as basic knowledge of the tradition of the laying on of hands. Perhaps my body is "wired" to have such flows more readily than most people's; perhaps I'm just the happy beneficiary of being more open to or conscious of the phenomenon; perhaps it was simply gratuitous grace.

What's important in the movie theater, I interpreted it not as a personal power, but as something almost anybody could experience. I felt it was potentially universal, but seldom allowed into consciousness, and certainly little talked about. With the danger of being dismissed as "woo-woo" or worse, I am trying to contribute to an intelligent discussion.

Photo by Kani Comstock of the author, taken during the period described in this book.

It is as if we are all in a conspiracy to limit ourselves to consensus reality, which is clearly a useful strategy for many purposes. By definition, we can share it. The trouble is, a marvelous experience may await on the other side of the boundary of ordinariness, outside the comfort zone.

When living in London the year after college, I used to walk from my flat in Bloomsbury across from the British Museum to Trafalgar Square. Most days, the square is full of tourists, occasionally a demonstration, with noisy red buses chugging along the edge and, over it all, Admiral Nelson perched on his column. On weekdays, a visitor heard only an urban din; but on Sunday mornings, the tranquil time, there emerged a chatter of birds. The birds were there all week, but they became audible only when the traffic thinned out.

In a similar way, I think our bodies contain initially hidden marvels of which we can remain unaware, or to which we can awaken; even if we awaken, as in my case, by surprise. Without dismissing theological interpretations, I am intrigued by the simplest possibility. Perhaps these phenomena are natural to the human brain and body, even though they are unlike our ordinary consensus reality. That would not mean we can "understand" how they are produced; it would simply mean we are willing to live with the mystery, without leaping to the hypothesis of a realm separate from human capacities.

Long after the evening when I watched *Koyaanisqatsi* for the second time, I noticed that at certain moments I would feel as if a woven lead apron, the kind they spread over your reproductive organs for a dental x-ray, were lifting off my head and shoulders. I hadn't noticed it was there until it was disappearing. At that point, a flow would start such that I no longer felt separate from the air above, to the sides, and eventually all around. On a physical level, it's obvious we are separate bodies. On the level of "flow," it can feel as if we're part of a larger field.

I did not interpret this experience of bliss as a result

of an "overactive imagination," or a sign of "spiritual achievement," whatever that is or, as in the Zen tradition, a kind of illusion that may draw a meditator away from valuable phenomena: "just keep sitting and it will go away."

It is true that bliss alone is not a life. As a book by Jack Kornfield says in its title, "after the ecstasy, the laundry." But what a huge joke it would be if happiness[4] (apart from the delights of fresh laundry) is not something you "attain" or "pursue," much less "merit," but something you "notice" or "let happen" or "get out of the way of."

Our culture is almost a machine for assuring that this noticing doesn't occur. Noticing may take leisure, not being eternally busy. It may require an openness to surprise, more than careful planning. It may take a kind of humility, not "attainment." It may require letting go, not accumulating (whether things or experience). It may be associated not with a solemn enhancement of the self ("ego psychology"), but perhaps with a sense of humor.

INEFFABILITY

Philosophers raise doubts about experiences that most of us assume that we obviously share: the clear sky is blue, heat cooks food, I kick a ball, being hit hurts. Most of us assume other people can understand when we tell stories, because the listener "resonates with" something that I have done or at least seen. We act as if other people know what it is to feel tired, happy, miserable, excited, angry.

Then there are experiences said to be ineffable,[5] indescribable, unutterable. As a book creation coach, I have often been in the position of assuring a client that "impossible" probably just means "hard," and urging him or her to make the effort to articulate, to find the words. I would tell him or her that, while challenging, the search for verbal expression is worth the effort. (Now I get to search for words.)

When talking about an experience that the listener hasn't had, or that was similar in some respects but very different in others, I can think of several approaches. You can identify a method that may allow the other person to have the experience. To take an eminent example, Buddha advised people to accept no dogma but to meditate and see for themselves where it leads. In the case of my experience in the movie theater and later, I can't do that because the state of being was spontaneous and I don't know a recipe that tells anybody else how to recreate it. I doubt that watching a movie directed by Godfrey Reggio will in general do the trick, or listening to a sound track composed by Philip Glass.

Another approach: you can try to enhance the self to which the experience happened, perhaps by becoming a teacher; but this risks building the ego even when one message of the experience is the costs of depending only on ego, however useful it is for navigating normal reality.

Or you can search for metaphors to describe the experience. Even if you cannot otherwise help people to create the experience, at least they will know, insofar as they credit your account, that the experience is humanly possible. If it begins, the listener is less likely to turn away from it or even deny it; more likely to go along with it and let the flower of it unfold. This is the method with which I'm left.

When over the course of months I told a few friends about the experience, I got reactions meant to be wise or at least cautionary. One person said such an experience could be dangerous without the guidance of a guru. Another dismissed it as meaning nothing. A third said the "energy" was "kundalini," a process of personal evolution described in Hindu thought. The kundalini power is said to be like a snake "sleeping" at the base of the spine, a snake that, awakened, ascends to the brain.

When I described the initial experience to the friend who typed my words, I was already speculating. In the theater, during the movie, "I tried to think of any energy about which I had ever heard or read that was at all like this. I thought of 'kundalini'.... I remember being told of warnings in some yoga books that awakening the kundalini without the proper preparation—some even said, without a guru— could lead to damage. And then I thought about R.D. Laing and his clients having experiences that he taught them to regard as healing journeys but that ordinary psychiatrists might have called psychotic breaks. At all times, I felt that mine was a healing journey...."

Long after that evening at the theater, I was told about Christina and Stan Grof's[6] "Spiritual Emergence Network." This was a group of practitioners trained to help people with disorienting experiences of something like what they called "transformational crisis." The Grofs came to the view that "some of the dramatic experiences and unusual states of mind that traditional psychiatry diagnoses and treats as mental diseases are actually ... 'spiritual emergencies'." They further note that "episodes of this kind have been described in sacred literature of all ages as a result of meditative practices and as signposts of the mystical path."

Traditional psychiatrists may have a prejudice very widely shared in our society, a prejudice against anything beyond the achievement of ordinary consensus reality. Or rather, not anything: it's okay, in the view of some observers, to invoke a spirit realm to "explain" unusual experience. What is less easily tolerated is the hypothesis that strong, unusual experience comes from unconscious parts of a sane mind.

We began by referring to the ineffable. Much of language

is based on a reality that we all presumably share and of which we are aware. Yes, we can imagine scenes that have never existed, as in fiction; and yes, we can imagine "ghosts" that have a different status than living people.

Perhaps the unconscious mind is even more fantastic than most of us give it credit for. We are unaware, except for some yogis, of the intricate regulation of the body. We are often astonished by our dreams: "where did *that* come from?" We can walk down the street, past a bookshop with thousands of novels, and believe people must have "past lives" because who could make up this stuff? Many humans define themselves as "uncreative" because the part of the mind that they know is hackneyed, but what do they harbor and not have access to?

Some experiences would become less "ineffable" if they were openly described—at least, as I have done, described roughly. Fear of being thought "woo-woo" is in some cases similar to taboos that have protected racism, sexism, and all the other discredited isms. What was once unthinkable becomes, after a turbulent period, taken for granted. I am white and male, but I don't need to treat non-whites and non-males as inferior in order to bolster my own worth. I am passably rational, but I don't need to deny or exile parts of the mind of which I'm not ordinarily aware.

SPIRITUAL BUT NOT RELIGIOUS

After the "Koya" experience, an acquaintance advised me to consider becoming a spiritual teacher. I found this a hilarious suggestion for several reasons, though, as a sometimes slow learner, it took me a while to realize an even deeper reason. My first and immediate objection was that I had nothing to teach, except to witness and report on a phenomenon: after all, the experience was spontaneous. I didn't do anything to bring it on: didn't sit on a pillow, get wise in any tradition, even wish for ecstasy.

What could I tell people? Write on a primitive desktop computer, get bored, go out for an ice-cream cone, wander into a movie with no plot and a minimalist sound track? When a barely discernible stirring begins in your foot, pay attention and let it build?

In my work as a book creation coach, I didn't like to lecture, preferring to ask questions and help clients grasp the truth that they were writing the books and needed to make thousands of decisions. All I was offering was encouragement, some awkward questions, and occasionally useful suggestions.

Thinking of leaders I had known, I also didn't like psychological projection, even positive, which, as I gathered from studies of group process, often turns negative. I didn't want to facilitate *any* projection, especially because the whole phenomenon of elevating exemplary people leaves the onlookers feeling small by comparison, unable to act: call it the fan club.

My third reason (is this enough?) was that an experience of bliss doesn't necessarily help one become more empathetic, more helpful, kinder; it may rather take one away from the suffering and doubts of life: as if to say, "why can't they be happy like me?"

At moments I attributed the experience to being wired a little unusually. Most of the time I think that bliss is a basic human experience, covered over by what we have learned to be in order to live in society and do the things that older kids and grownups do.

There seemed a relation between "Koya" and my interest in "autotelic" or "ludic" experience, which some academic colleagues considered a strange topic for a doctoral program.

Perhaps I gravitated to a preoccupation with play because I was too serious as a child.

This dated, at least in part, from leafing through a photo magazine in my best friend's living room. This would have been in the mid-1950s. An article described the effects of an atomic bomb dropped on Times Square. I realized that, depending on the time of day, a bomb there would obliterate my Dad, who worked just a few blocks away, in sight of the main branch of the New York Public Library.

I didn't shy away from becoming a spiritual teacher for lack of models. For example, my girl friend and I went to see a teacher later associated with a magazine called *What Is Enlightenment?* She had been a "sanyassin" in the group started by Bhagwan Shree Rajneesh.

This brings us to a delicate subject. Nietzsche told his readers that God was dead, but especially for a young western audience, God got an extension by assuming Eastern forms. Without feeling a need to deny this sort of faith, I found it life enhancing to imagine "spiritual" experiences as natural to humans as we'd evolved, without the further need to posit a divine realm.

Here was my fourth reason for not becoming a teacher. I knew nothing better than experiences labeled as "spiritual," which, however, I regarded, in the absence of evidence to the contrary, as a natural, human capacity. Think of it as a working hypothesis, a starting point.

"Spiritual" experience is so different from ordinary experience that it's natural to assume it comes from a separate realm, of which we may have no other evidence except that many people, in many cultures, have made that assumption. But then, many people once thought the sun revolved around the earth or that the earth was flat. Many people accepted philosophies that successors argued were wrong. Before Einstein, many people thought that Newton was the last word in physics.

I'd like to encourage experience that's "outside the box," without its being quickly and anxiously relegated to categories called either "religious" or "psychotic." What about the possibility of a graceful weaving between ordinary reality, which is useful for many purposes, and other kinds of human experience?

On internet dating sites, I am told that hopeful people often now describe themselves as "spiritual but not religious." What does this mean? In some cases, I suspect it means, "I'm no longer a churchgoer but don't want you to assume I'm just a callow materialist" or "I'm open to phenomena that we don't understand." What I mean is closer to the latter, but I'd not say only "I'm open to" but add "I highly value." I highly value certain experiences for which I don't necessarily hope to achieve a scientific understanding.

Yes, I regret not being able to have a hypothesis confirmed by independent experiment, or not falsified as Karl Popper would have said (during the year that I was enrolled at the London School of Economics, I audited Popper's class on the philosophy of science). Despite the advances made recently in neurology, for example, even techniques such as functional magnetic resonance imaging supply data that will some day seem crude, but which is meanwhile marvelous. We have learned much about the brain, for example, from head injuries, from tiny probes in the brain, and from the MRI, but these technologies barely touch the kinds of phenomena I'm talking about.

Meanwhile, we have the choice of either ignoring or making up stories about phenomena that we don't understand, or, as I'd suggest, simply describing it as best we can.

OUT-OF-BODY

If you had asked me, in the middle of my life, to search out somebody with a mystical experience, I would not have started in my immediate family. My father was an electrical engineer, who spread out blueprints on the dining table between meals and who asked me, when I was still a teenager, to disambiguate the language that his committee of leading fellow engineers had found for the new U.S. code for electrical power handling. My mother had been a commonsensical Milwaukee girl, raised in the Lutheran church, a follower of her home state's senator Joseph McCarthy when I was growing up.

Decades later, when I was in my late forties and my father had died, I had the notion of interviewing my mother about her life, and showed up for a visit with a tape recorder. She played along. In this setting she told me about an episode that she'd never hinted at, much less recounted to any of her children. The events happened when I was a baby, then an only child, before the appearance of my sister Kani a little more than two years after my own birth.

Unknowingly, my mother had an ectopic pregnancy, which I much later learned in her case meant a fetus growing not in the womb but in a fallopian tube (which leads from an ovary to the uterus). The growing fetus stresses or bursts the tube, causing a hemorrhage.

According to my mother, when she began bleeding, her doctor was off duty, and not eager to interrupt his time at the golf club until my aunt, the head nurse at a Milwaukee hospital, suggested rather strongly that he meet my mother and her at the hospital as soon as possible.

My mother was put on a gurney and was wheeled immediately into an operating room. Lying there, before receiving anesthesia, she became conscious of a loving presence behind her head, and looking back she saw an angel. When she later told her pastor about this experience, he thanked her for sharing this story but said it might be best if she never spoke of it again.

My mother knew the figure was an angel, because it had wings, as in Italian Renaissance paintings of which she later grew fond. The angel was a man (this was decades prior to the feminism of the 1970s). He told her not to worry, that he would take care of her.

But she then noticed a hole in an upper corner of the operating room and thought, "this is rather unsanitary." The hole opened into a glowing tunnel, toward which she began to float.

Hearing this, as the tape recorder turned, I thought, "oh yes, an out-of-body experience,[7] just like in the books." I later found that she'd never heard of the concept of an OBE, and realized, in any case, the relevant books had been written long after she had the experience.

Floating, she suddenly thought that she couldn't leave her young husband or her baby (me), so she felt that she willed her way back to the gurney. Then somebody put a mask over her face and the next she knew, she was waking up in a hospital room. Meanwhile, her husband, hearing from the surgeon that she might not make it, had fainted in a corridor. (Her baby was at home, being cared for by the aunt who was a nurse.)

My mother lived to the age of 94. She had three more children, raised them largely in a New York City suburb, traveled extensively in this country, in Europe, and in East Asia.

Without passing judgment on reports of OBEs, I just want to note that hers was in the idiom of the Christianity in which she was raised (angels with wings, a chimera of humans and birds) and that her pastor, uncomfortable with a living example of an experience we call "mystical," gave typical and probably sage advice. Her OBE was among the most important experiences of her life but not to be talked about (except decades later, in a formal interview, conducted by a son).

After hearing this report, I left wondering how many other experiences are left unspoken, because people are afraid other people will regard them as (even if only momentarily) crazy. Hearing her story, I was so amazed it didn't occur to me to ask whether she'd ever shared this story with her husband. (It's one of the 10,000 things that I would like to know but just don't.)

Paradoxically, the present availability of reports of OBEs may confuse future accounts, at least among people who read them or discuss them. People who have seen something out of the ordinary may wonder to what extent they are recalling a pattern that they read about and overlaid on the experience. That is why I was so excited to learn my mother's relation to published accounts: they were unavailable when she had the emergency surgery, and in any case never heard of the subsequent research.

This innocence doesn't mean the events in her report necessarily describe a phenomenon outside the mind of, in this case, my mother. Perhaps when life is threatened, humans have hallucinations of escaping this dangerous realm and passing through a tunnel to a better world. But this itself would be an astonishing fact of life, not to be hidden and, I would add, not necessarily to be attributed hastily to a transcendental realm.

Hearing this account left me feeling closer to my mother. It was clearly more important to her consciousness than her pride about the number of times she could swim the

Milwaukee River as an adolescent or, later, her initially reluctant move to the wilds of the New York metropolitan area or the surprises that children bring. I did not share all of her beliefs, but did admire, among other qualities, her willingness to value a vision. And to describe it.

5

Family Dynamics

Fear of pain blinds us to the goal of healing. Only by seeing our problems clearly and experiencing them can we do something about them. There really is a way to arrive at something better than life as we may have known it, no matter how completely we may have given in to despair—even if only periodically. There is a way out. Others have done it and gone on to lives of fulfillment and peace….

– BOB HOFFMAN, *No One Is To Blame*

Like many other adventures of mine in the 1980s, it was as a book creation coach that I first heard of the Hoffman Quadrinity Process.[1] The founder, Bob Hoffman,[2] sought my help in revising his book on Quadrinity (this term refers to what he regards as the four aspects of being human).

In order to give good advice, I felt it was necessary not only to read his book but also to experience at least some of the process. Okay, he said, "buy a plastic bat and a tough pillow and I will take you to a session this evening." At that time, the Process was given once a week, stretching over several months.

We drove from Berkeley to the peninsula south of San Francisco, not far from the airport, but obviously a luxurious neighborhood. The meeting was held in a large building behind the house. As the group gathered I gazed at a mural filling one end of the room. The mural depicted angels, including, our host said, his own mother.

After some talk, we were requested to regard our pillows (mine was dark green nylon) as if they were patterns adopted in childhood from our parents and to begin beating the life out of these subconscious patterns. We were told to take out the aggression we presumably felt but which we could not, as children, safely enact then or of which we might not even later become conscious. Soon the room was like bedlam.

My first impression of the "process" was not favorable. It seemed nothing more than the expression, popular at the time, of anger against somebody, whether parents, men, the society, or the enemy. I wanted to leave. The contrast between the painted angels and the screaming members of the group was grotesque. What good could come of acting like a mob hunting down parents who, if alive, were probably old and defenseless? In most cases surely they'd done the best they knew how.

However, I was intrigued enough to take the job of helping the founder revise his book, knowing that I could try to recollect the scene in tranquility, that the process included much more than the mock beatings I had witnessed, and that I could help the author describe what he had discovered. I knew, too, that we were beating not representations of our parents, but of specific patterns that we'd identified.

The more I learned about the Hoffman Process, the more necessary and effective it seemed. At first I thought it would be enough to watch others go through all or part of the workshop, but soon realize I had to do it for myself, as a participant not only as a spectator.

The process had meanwhile been shifted into a residential format taking one very intensive week. The setting was a ranch north of San Francisco Bay, with drafty board-and-batten cabins. After a winter night, we defrosted in front of little electric heaters and, in the dining hall, a big fireplace.

My teacher, one of the staff, was a former Unitarian minister. With the help of a guidebook, the teachers read various visualizations, asked questions, talked about how it was to be kids. Before arriving we had done elaborate homework, read in advance by the teachers, who had individual sessions with their small circles of students.

Accomplished largely with the whole group in the big room, the process was curiously private. One of the rules was that no student would comment on another or try to "help." The exchanges were all between student and teachers. The most sensitive material was saved for the individual sessions. People were identified only by their child names, not by who they had become. I was just "Craig," with nothing said about my formal education, my profession, my work in the world.

The process is described in general terms in *Journey Into Love*, a book later co-written by one of my sisters, Kani Comstock, who also later helped to revise and update the process that she and a colleague then explained. The work begins with an elaborate catalogue of lessons learned from each parent, then with a symbolic beating of negative patterns adopted from each parent, followed by a surprise move, deep compassion for her and for him.

The earlier expression of rage is not lessened or modified by premature forgiveness, which comes only after the anger is fully expressed. As in the South African "truth and reconciliation" commission, the ugly truth is exposed before the parties are ready for any degree of tolerance or empathy.

After blaming parents for negative patterns adopted in childhood, participants are taught to grasp that parents, too, adopted patterns they were too young to understand or resist, patterns too unconscious later to be seen and evaluated without help.

As my yoga teacher and friend had introduced me to painting, as one early client had alerted me to spiritual experience, as Margo had shown me the way of tantra, my client Bob drew me into a process that he had developed. I thus learned about unconscious imprinting from parents, and how to go beyond it.

Each of these activities was initially strange to me. Whatever success I had experienced in life was as an intellectual, not an artist, or more generally what Jungians call a feeling-type. Prior to the shocks described above, I was much more interested in science than in anything called spiritual. I'd never heard of tantra. Many of my feelings toward parents were unresolved even when not wholly unconscious. But after venturing into these worlds, following clients, I did not want to imagine life without these other ways of being.

PATTERNS

The very concept of the unconscious seems to subvert the Enlightenment hope that human behavior is or could be governed by rationality. To what extent is our life ruled by impulses and patterns of which we're not necessarily even aware? It's hard to change patterns about which don't know except, we're told, through such oblique sources as dreams, wit, slips of the tongue, free association. Hard, but not impossible. According to Bob Hoffman, it's even possible to identify and change patterns much more quickly than through traditional "analysis" or other gradual techniques.

As founder of the Hoffman Process, Bob came to believe that people are largely run by patterns adopted in childhood in order to assure the love of parents (and their surrogates), patterns of which the children were often not conscious. Adopted by whom? By dependent children whose first task is to assure the support of their protectors. To do so, the best strategy often seems to be appearing similar to the protectors. Bob called this "negative love." "I'm just like you," it's as if the child is saying, "now will you love me?"

Bob felt that most adults are run by these patterns, which may once have been useful, but which, in the changed situation of adulthood, are usually a drag. Clearly, the first step is to become aware of the patterns; then, to get free of them and replace them.

But how?

The method developed by Bob took months to do in the format of one meeting per week; and starting in 1985 a week to do in an intensive residential process during which students did nothing else but eat and, when possible, sleep. The week is conceived not as "therapy," but as education. On the one side of the room are teachers, who have done both the process for themselves and then a program of training; on the other side, students who, as noted, do not comment on each other, but focus wholly on their own work.

I was drawn to this process not as a "workshop junkie" but as a writing coach who felt I should experience what my client had created and was describing. At first I thought it would be enough to watch others go through all or part of the workshop, but soon realized I had to do it for myself.

In his persona as an arrogant right-wing commentator, blinded by ideology, the comedian Stephen Colbert says that he doesn't care whether you are Muslim, Hindu, Christian, Buddhist, or whatever: "there are many paths to acceptance of Jesus as your savior." People who benefit from a particular workshop tend to assume both that it's relevant to everybody and that it's the one true path. I don't feel that way.

I have seen the Hoffman Process not make as dramatic a difference as its teachers hope; and have also seen friends benefit from other methods. However, it's worth a close look. (The Process is available not only in the U.S., but also in Canada and in Latin America, including Brazil and Argentina, in Australia, and in several European countries.)

Listing here the negative patterns that I had adopted would not help anyone else, but exploring a few positive patterns might. For example, curiosity. I know that many of us live by the observation, "curiosity killed the cat." But the cat has nine lives. It's true that curiosity can get cats into trouble, but so, in many circumstances, can human incuriosity. (I learned this word from Eric Larrabee, an editor at *American Heritage* where I had the good fortune to spend the summer after college. EL, as he signed the evaluation sheets we passed around about submissions, was a model of curiosity.)

From which parent did I get the curiosity that I try to follow? The answer is from both. As an engineer, my father was not only a salesman but also an inventor. He was happiest when he discovered a need that wasn't met by anything on the market and then could create an electrical device that worked. He did so with the ground fault detector, which, so Kani says, made it possible to put many electric lines underground rather than on poles.

My mother loved educating herself, especially after her parents declined to send her to college, as they had done for her brothers. She learned about her religion (teaching Sunday school), about nutrition (listening to the radio, reading books), about curricula (campaigning in school board elections, having a psychologist friend), about interior design (books again, designing furniture built by her father, attending a leading Manhattan school), and about real estate (starting a career in her sixties).

The strength of the Hoffman Process came, I think, from its unwillingness either to stop at blaming parents or to attempt premature reconciliation. In the words of the founder, "everyone is guilty but no one is to blame." The truth had to be acknowledged in detail, but only as a first step. The goal is to reach a nuanced judgment, in a frame of compassion and resolution.

In the next two units I want to share what I learned about my parents. I have already written about my father's last stage: here I want to tell a little about his earlier life, and in particular, about his relation to curiosity. And so far I have not written about my mother at all. I want to say a little about her growing cosmopolitanism. The Hoffman Process offers an alternative to both blame and shallow praise. Here is some of what I came to understand about my own parents as a result of the process founded by a client. Again, while the details of my life are unimportant here, they suggest a certain attitude, which may help in meeting challenges.

DAD

After growing up on a farm in southern Minnesota, my father became an engineer. He did not feel I should be bound to his profession, any more than he had been to his father's work growing corn and hay and keeping livestock (cows, sheep, chickens). He felt each child should choose his or her own life, not necessarily follow the parents. At various stages he accepted my passion for being an attorney and public servant, a college teacher, a foundation executive, an editor and writer.

When at the age of ten I saw and lusted after a blue Schwinn bicycle, he said, "That's great. I will pay for half.

Now let's figure out how you can earn the rest." And he'd draw out of me schemes to sell extension cords or garden seeds in our neighborhood. I got the bike. He'd give advice mainly by asking questions, as Plato had helped a slave boy reinvent geometry (though I didn't read the ancient Greek philosopher until age eighteen).

Dad had two great faults. Losing his temper without warning, he would occasionally and suddenly get furious. In one incident, Mom pulled him off me, pulled so hard she tore the shirt off his back, saying she'd leave him if he ever spanked a child again. The other fault was a tendency to start a complex job without all the necessary tools or supplies, and then impatiently rely on his helper (often me) to fetch in increments whatever turned out to be relevant. At worst, he was volatile, scatter-brained, or both.

But he clearly cared about the family. He would spend long times focusing on our problems, was a good teacher (even of driving), provided well for us, and best of all, taught some good values by quiet example.

I was shocked when I saw a wedding portrait of my parents. My mother looks confident, even glamorous; my father, not quite ready for prime time. He seems younger than she was, in spite of being a little older. I suppose it had been almost a culture shock to go from the farm to a Big Ten university, from being a good student (even in ROTC) to working in a big engineering company, and later from life in the Midwest to the Northeast.

He was proud of having bright kids. When his other son began getting low grades in math, he went to see the teacher who, it turned out, couldn't understand how Bruce was getting the correct answer without going through the proper steps on paper. (He did the problems in his head.)

The older of my sisters, Kani, thought of herself as the

slow one: even after being one of the first women in her graduate department of biology at our father's university, she became director of a Japanese-owned school in Tokyo, learning the language, after which she became a kind of therapist (they called her a "teacher") in the Hoffman Process, then an author, twice, so far. The third child, Bruce, studied economics, programmed early computers, then started his life in the air as a champion hot air balloonist. Our younger sister Barbara got started by learning Chinese, earning a master of fine arts, making some soft sculpture that's shown in books, living in Katmandu and trekking in the Himalayas.

Dad could respond quickly in emergencies. For example, when one of the kids left the faucet running in the tub located above the front hall and the tub overflowed, he realized the plaster ceiling could collapse from the weight of the flood, ran to the basement for a power drill and, calling for pots and bowels, punched holes in the ceiling. He then washed off the plaster dust and returned to the dining table.

He was quick-witted, too. Once Dad absent-mindedly put heavy cream on his Sunday supper waffles and the maple syrup in his coffee, insisting humorously, after the slightest of lags, that this was a valuable if accidental invention. "You haven't lived," he said, "until you've had cream on your waffles."

Sometimes we kids would go too far, as when I was in junior high and my brother in the upper reaches of grade school. We gathered our quarters and took the train south into New York City to attend a matinee of a play by Brendan Behan. In town, the playwright had a bit too much to drink with lunch and stumbling down the aisle during the performance, he recited the lines along with the characters and generally created a nuisance. The actors pulled him up on stage and hustled him into the wings. Apparently it wasn't the first time.

Afterward I led my brother backstage to congratulate the playwright, which I must have thought was a grown-up thing to do. Actors encouraged us to support Behan out a side door and down the alley to a waiting cab. Unfortunately, somebody had alerted one of the tabloids, which sent a photographer. The next morning the newspaper ran a front page photo of two boys helping the drunken playwright into a cab. Our father saw it at the train station and put the kabosh on any future expeditions to the big city without adults.

The message was always double: we'd gone too far, but enterprise was admirable. To explore and innovate was good.

A KIND OF IMMIGRANT

As I have described, stage one of the Hoffman Process involved "bashing" the patterns we each absorbed from parents, patterns that had remained largely unconscious and, the teachers said ominously, governed much of our lives. Stage two brought us to compassion for these people, but only after an expression of informed and focused rage.

While "bashing," participants each had his or her own way of breaking through, of going "over the top" into physical anger. Mine turned out to be a hallucination of Mom sitting on the side on a familiar bentwood kitchen chair, watching me bash half-heartedly and deploying one of her favorite sayings, "what about the last ten percent?" That did it.

In the next stage of the process I realized that, to some degree, my parents had suffered as immigrants in the New York metro area. The family had come not from Germany (except decades before on my mother's side) or Japan (though one of my sisters later married a Japanese scientist), but only from Milwaukee. We were U.S. citizens. We grew up speaking English. Even in the Depression, my father had a good job. But from my mother's point of view (and to some extent my father's), they'd left the old country (the Midwest) and landed in an alien place (the New York City area). This was in the early 1940s.

The move began innocently: my father's company, which made electrical switches, sent him on a temporary trip to New York City to figure out how to fix the controls on some U.S. Navy ships that were being dispatched, on "lend-lease," to an increasingly desperate United Kingdom. He succeeded and the New York office asked him to stay. So the rest of the family went east on a train called the Twentieth Century Limited. I was pre-school; my sister, a baby.

My mother arrived with a mixed heritage. Proud later that Golda Meir had taught in Milwaukee schools before becoming an Israeli and then prime minister, my mother was also proud of Milwaukee as a German city displaced, as it were, to the western shore of Lake Michigan. She admired German virtues of precision, hard work, order, and as the sociologist C. Wright Mills once said, "good motors." She was so oblivious that some of her ancestor's people could misbehave big time that, when I once stopped by her house with a Jewish friend, she praised German virtues, unaware that not everyone had a good experience of that country. (My friend just murmured, "hmm.")

Mom's parents had experienced nationalist prejudice during the Great War, when a neighbor began gossiping about the "Krauts" across the street. Her mother knocked on their door and asked how long their family had been Americans, and being told, made clear that hers had been here longer: they were Americans, not Krauts. I like the story, but not for measuring loyalty by length of time on this continent. Franklin D. Roosevelt, from a Dutch family that came early to the Hudson Valley, began an address to the Daughters of the American Revolution[3] by saluting them as "fellow immigrants!" (Except for the early tribes and some recent air-borne arrivals, we're all boat people.)

I think my mother was in awe of New York City. We lived in the suburbs (briefly in Flushing, mainly to the north in White Plains). Later she'd ride the train south to help her husband entertain customers (a Dodgers game, a dinner, or a Broadway show). Our parents took us to the great museums on either side of Central Park (Natural History on the west, the Metropolitan on the east). In Rockefeller Center we'd see movies, watch ice skaters, be dazzled (and at our age, a little puzzled) by the high-kicking Rockettes.

When I got a letter announcing my admission to Harvard, I was too excited to notice an ambivalence on my mother's part. She and my father had agreed that all their children would attend college, girls as well as boys, as was not the case in her generation.

I discovered the source of her hesitation when she delivered me to work one day in the summer before freshman year, near a warehouse where I helped load boxes of books off of trucks and, after orders were filled, onto other trucks. As she left me off, she said, "I'm so sorry you're going to Harvard because it means you will probably go to hell." As I later learned, some parents went to great lengths to get their offspring into "good" colleges, which they didn't associate with eternal ill fortune in an afterlife.

Fortunately, having no satisfactory reply, I had to rush off to be on time. I did not have occasion to say that any switch in my beliefs would not come as a result of attending a secular college, but had already happened while attending a boarding high school run by her church. In any case, her other kids went to midwestern or mountain state colleges, though I'm not sure that assured religious propriety.

After I had edited a pair of books and worked for five years with a foundation that had the goal of helping to end the Cold War (described in Chapters 6 and 7), I had lunch with my mother, then a real estate agent in the San Francisco Bay Area. She asked when I was going to "settle down and get a real job." I inquired what she had in mind. "Selling houses," she said. I'm not sure she ever appreciated what I was doing at the foundation or, before and after, as a book creation coach working with authors.

In contrast, two of her children were employed in or had started a business, my first sister as director of English as a Second Language schools both in Tokyo and in the San Francisco Bay Area, my brother as the principal, with his wife, in a company manufacturing hot air balloons. In Mom's view, this was real, as shown by such markers as cash flow, employees, commissions, inventory, and profit. Working for some cause or helping somebody behind the scenes, as physicians or psychotherapists do, was less so.

My mother gradually became an Easterner and more cosmopolitan. Because her first daughter had a job in international exchange that required frequent trips to East Asia, my mother once got to go on a tour of China. When the train would pull into a big city, officials would be there to greet the delegation, and because our mother was the oldest, they often assumed she was the visiting dignitary. After accepting the reception she'd always felt she deserved, she would graciously pass the Chinese on to her daughter, who was the exchange official.

ADVENTURES

If Dad was the engineer, Mom was the artist. After school she hadn't painted (unlike my wife Shoshanah). Mom channeled her artistic gifts into interior design.

Through all of my childhood at home, Mom was not allowed to work: "no wife of mine has to slave for a paycheck," said my young father. Later, she concocted a scheme involving my youngest sibling, who, she argued, just had to attend an exclusive and expensive private school in Westchester County where we lived. Who would earn the extra money? Why, she would, by attending the New York School of Interior Design and working, initially, for a fancy Manhattan department store.

The school my younger sister attended was the kind where students sail with classmates on warm-weather weekends, and learn lacrosse, not bowling. This scheme worked. With regard to having his wife work, Dad had meanwhile been softened up by the social movements of the 60s.

Earlier Mom made a beautiful home in which to grow up. She was helped in this by her father, a woodworker, with whom she designed furniture to be built in fruit or nut woods or mahogany.

To my taste, the best of all her efforts was the dining room. In the middle was a walnut table big enough for the parents and four kids, set with Duncan Phyfe-style chairs made by her father. Over the table hung a brass chandelier out of some Dutch genre painting. On one side, a cabinet for dishes with glass front, also built by her father; and facing it a large window to the front yard and a mature maple tree.

Like any child, I regarded whatever existed as normal. I did notice that one of the art reproductions in the living room showed a Dutch couple soberly counting gold coins on a Persian carpet flung over a table. They seemed unembarrassed by their prosperity: careful, almost worshipful.

Mom stood up for her values even when they caused pain or puzzlement to others (regretting that a son was going to Harvard). She blossomed first as a mother (how hard it must be to raise four boisterous kids), then as a professional. Mom had three careers, as a "homemaker," as an interior designer, and as a real estate salesperson. She was especially proud of being invited, by the college system in California, to teach interior design. The woman who had not been sent to college became a professor.

When my father had to go into a nursing home, she asked whether I'd drive her furniture east, helping to load a rental truck, and then to unload it in Ann Arbor. I replied I would if she would keep me company in the cab. Here I saw more about her sense of adventure.

In Arizona we glimpsed a faded sign about an enormous crater and, after looking at one another, drove the truck off on a narrow and desolate road through the desert. After several ridges it ended in a parking lot next to a low building. Entering, we saw on the far side a crater a half-mile wide, created by a chunk of metal that fell at enormous speed and displaced all that dirt and rock. We could have been on the moon. In fact, a sign told us that NASA used the crater for training purposes.

Crossing the Mississippi in flood, we stopped at an all-you-can-eat restaurant in East St. Louis and went through the buffet line. Famished earlier in the day, my mother stuffed into her big purse pieces of crusty chicken on which we could later gnaw. The restaurant was the sort of place where, after you got your food in the buffet line, a waitress came to the table to take orders for drinks. At that point, my mother's bulging purse sprang open, and a drumstick popped out onto the table.

Going through Ohio, we saw a sign about an air force museum and abruptly turned off, as we had for the crater. In a hanger, at the end of a long hall, I saw a replica of "Fat Man," the plutonium atom bomb dropped on Nagasaki.

The point of all these stories is surprise. Sometimes we were embarrassed (but the waitress joined our laughter about the purloined chicken), sometimes awed (Arizona crater, Ohio bomb). But always, as Mom used to say, we "rolled with the punches."

As a kid, to judge by the stories, I was a challenge. I once fell off the top of the refrigerator. My mother used to say "he'd walk across the ceiling if he could." This didn't make life easier for those around me, but the message I got was that while normalness was valued, it was mainly as a background for riffs.

Helping a Little
to End a War

6

Ark

In the words of the old black spiritual, "God gave Noah the rainbow sign—no more water, the fire next time." Instead of trying to find a little place where we could be sheltered against a possible holocaust, we must now think of the whole earth as the new ark. Our task now is to build an imaginary vessel big enough to encompass all mankind, an ark as big as the earth itself.

– DON CARLSON, in Citizen Summitry: Keeping the Peace When It Matters Too Much to be Left to Politicians

At first, ventures outside my comfort zone took the form of internal experience or relationship with one or two people, such as a partner, a client, or my parents. I engaged in no political activity. Then I was invited to take a leading role in a new foundation with the single aim of helping to end the Cold War.

I never would have taken the job, which at first struck me as a folly, if I had not been surprised and educated by the earlier personal lessons. What I learned is that our assumptions about what is possible are typically much too narrow. I also knew that personal development, by itself, is not enough.

After ecstatic experience and family dynamics, I found myself immersed in global politics. The story begins with a question during a long car ride, with the Cuban missile crisis, and with a made-for-TV movie.

During college I had some acquaintance with ideas about nuclear strategy advanced by local talent such as Henry Kissinger *(Nuclear Weapons and Foreign Policy)* and Tom Schelling *(The Strategy of Conflict)*. However, my most memorable encounter was with a Harvard divinity student who gave me a ride, in his red Volvo, from my hometown of White Plains, New York, to Cambridge, Massachusetts.

Near the start of the ride he asked me, "if you were President and the U.S. were in the process of being attacked by nuclear bombs, would you then, under those circumstances, give the order to retaliate?" (Perhaps he had been asked this very question in an ethics class.) "Well," he said after I'd puzzled silently for a while, "what would be the point? Kill 100 million or more innocent people for nothing except revenge? Wreck the remaining half of the northern hemisphere?"

Obviously, however, the system of deterrence depended on a credible threat of retaliation, whether it was a second strike or, more riskily, a strike on suspicion the USSR was about to attack. President Nixon was right when he observed that it was helpful, in this situation, to seem a bit crazy. If you wouldn't retaliate, and if that were known, your country might be wrecked. You had to appear tough or even, as Nixon said, a little insane. (The other side had to worry that, in a crisis, you might act irrationally, be caught up in the dynamics of the challenge.)

I thought of this terrible quandary when reading Chapter 2 of Jonathan Schell's *The Unconquerable World,* which concerns the Cuban missile crisis.

Once the opponent has a reliable second strike capacity, the only rational course is to avoid an "exchange." There was a period when the U.S. had many ICBMs and the Soviets didn't, when our military could have struck first and "accepted" the Soviet bombs that nonetheless would be launched or dropped. But at what cost? Washington? New York? Chicago?

Schell tells of former Secretary of State Dean Acheson advising a President that he should decide, in advance, what to do if attacked and then not tell anyone. The only reason not to tell anyone would be if you had decided *not* to retaliate. As Schell notes, Acheson felt he couldn't say this outright, even in a private meeting.

Like the picture magazine I'd seen as a child at my best friend's house, the one showing the effects of a nuclear bomb exploding in midtown Manhattan, the conversation with the divinity student stayed with me as we then lived through the Cuban missile crisis in October 1962 and subsequent military adventures.

We'll never know whether JFK would have shown the caution and forbearance he did during the Cuban missile crisis if he had never read Barbara Tuchman's *Guns of August*,[1] which is about the start of the First World War (or, as it was then known, the Great War). But I remember the first exercise in our history tutorial at college. We were assigned to read various sources and then explain how the war of 1914 began, or rather, why. It turned out to be impossible. As an Austrian official is said to have declared, at the time, "the situation is tragic but not serious." In other words, millions will die, but we don't quite know why.

THE DAY AFTER

In 1983, I was impressed by a TV movie that showed the results, in a Midwest city, of a nuclear attack. The movie was called *The Day After*.[2] It was seen by more than 100 million people during its initial broadcast on ABC.

There had been other movies about nuclear war, including *On the Beach* (1959) and *Dr. Strangelove* (1964), but neither of those movies showed ordinary folks, in the U.S. heartland, trying to survive in radioactive rubble. The first movie was set in Australia and aboard a sub, with brief excursions into U.S. coastal installations; the second, a black comedy, took place largely on "Burpleson AFB" and in the U.S. war room, prior to an unstoppable attack on the USSR plotted by a renegade SAC officer. The last scene shows a cowboy pilot riding a nuclear bomb as it falls, as if it were his horse, waving his Stetson, with the sound track playing "We'll meet again, don't know where, don't know when."

In contrast, *The Day After* was deadly serious in tone. Broadcast on TV, it must have helped a large sector of the population to emerge at least partway out of denial or ignorance. (President Reagan had a private screening and, despite being a professional optimist, was depressed.) The English lift an eyebrow at the supposed American distaste for understatement, but a U.S. bumper sticker of the time read, "A nuclear war can ruin your whole day." On network TV *The Day After* showed just how bad that could look.

It was not until 2007 that Henry Kissinger joined with some of his colleagues to write about the dangers of nuclear weapons, but long before that, President Reagan had continued the very gradual and limited pullback from the nuclear arms race begun by JFK. There were many influences on Reagan, including a persistent anti-nuclear weapons movement, but I imagine that a big influence was a growing sense among ordinary voters that the national security elites were playing a dangerous game, in which the potential damage was vastly greater than in the terrible war they knew as young people, and that the danger did not have to be as great as it was.

DON

I was introduced to Don Carlson as a book creation coach and told that he'd been raised in a simple home, gone to Stanford on an athletic scholarship, and then found work supervising playgrounds and selling life insurance. One of his friends was a young lawyer. At a breakfast, one of them had the idea of selling shares in a portfolio of many buildings, but the other raised doubts, observing that people who buy real estate like to "kick brick" (even if ownership is evidenced by a piece of paper). The person with the idea (as good collaborators, they won't say who it was) suggested they try one limited partnership, which then had tax advantages. If the partnership didn't work, they'd move on.

Cover of Citizen Summitry, *edited by Carlson & Comstock*

When I met Don in 1984, their company owned the equivalent of a U.S. city, though the shopping centers, office buildings, and apartments were spread out geographically.

As we're taught to say, Don was personally "worth" $90 million, a modest amount according to today's standards set by multi-billionaires, but enough, as they say in those circles, to feel "comfortable."

At our first lunch, Don told me he was in his early fifties, and could go on piling up the money, or he could do something socially useful with his life. I suppose it was a bit like Steve Jobs asking the CEO of one of the cola companies, do you want to sell sugar water the rest of your life or do you want to help lead a revolution? In any case, I found Don's attitude refreshing.

It turned out that he wanted to start a foundation and write a book. Meanwhile, he was working with other entrepreneurs and managers in a group called Business Executives for National Security (BENS), which critiqued "waste, fraud, and abuse" in the military-industrial complex.

I learned that Don had a reputation for going to breakfast with the heads of various local non-profits and making generous personal grants. By the time these directors finished their Spanish omelets, their organizations were richer than when they had ordered.

In starting the Ark Foundation and "communications institute," Don replaced this genial local style with a single and global goal, helping to end the Cold War. He felt that unless we no longer had superpowers threatening to destroy each other, the risk of accident or miscalculation was too high to tolerate. I accepted the job, first to help edit the books, then to work for Ark. We began looking for allies and forms of action.

Of course our goal seemed ridiculous. By that time, the Cold War had lasted at least thirty-five years. People on both sides assumed it was almost a natural feature of the world, like oxygen in the air, fish in the sea, ice in the Arctic.

"Containment" would last for the foreseeable future: what could possibly change the need for that policy? Hearing our goal, friends in effect patted us on the head and said that at least we'd probably do no harm.

Don figured he had nothing to lose. Like many rich people, he had more homes than he could occupy, and less time for his boat than he felt that it deserved. He wanted something more than to expand a wildly successful company. Quaintly, he wanted to apply entrepreneurial skills to public policy.

As we worked together, I quickly morphed from being a writing coach to being a partner in the enterprise, and the book turned into a pair, with many contributors. We were delighted when Jeremy Tarcher decided to publish the books (the firm that he founded in Los Angeles is now an imprint of Penguin), and earlier when the vice chair of the Soviet Academy of Sciences helped us find some Soviet contributors, who, in place of any party line, would join our array of Western writers in envisioning a world after the Cold War.

It was natural that, even before the books were wholly edited, Carlson invited me to join the foundation and communications institute. In one sense, I was an employee. In another sense, typical of Carlson, he offered to consider me as an equal partner, as if he weren't putting up all the money. It was 1984. He wanted a commitment for no more and no less than five years. In 1989, with a theatrical appropriateness, the Berlin Wall was broken through, and soon the Soviet Union was splitting into Russia and nearby states.

I was able to turn my attention to Ark because I worked with only a few clients at a time, and Don gave me time to finish other projects before reporting for work. This was a dream job, investing in change agents after editing the pair of books for which we then did an extensive publicity tour.

BETTER AT WAR

Don and I were often asked, why not just stand aside and let governments handle foreign relations? Here's how I replied in one of our books.[3]

> Citizen summitry is the application of individual initiative to what are normally considered the highest matters of state—relations with an adversary. As an ordinary citizen you engage in summitry not by wangling an invitation to the next meeting with Gorbachev, but by deciding that peace matters too much to be left only to politicians. Of course politicians will always be central to any decisions about war, defense, and "national security"; it is they, with diplomats and military officers, who negotiate treaties, make alliances, take actions affecting the terms of international trade, and deploy armed forces. But in our fascination with this ruling elite, magnified as they are by the contemporary media, we may easily forget our own sources of creativity.
>
> Fifty-four percent of our citizens agree with the statement that "when it comes to America's national security, the President has access to secret information and we should go along with what he decides." Fifty-six percent say that "the idea of nuclear war is so horrible, I try not to think about it." And what is the result of going along with the national security apparatus and of turning away from any independent thought about the nuclear danger? Thirty-eight percent of Americans believe that the "likelihood of nuclear war is the next ten years is

(very or fairly) great." This statistic staggers me. It says that, on the average, if I'm in a checkout line with four other people, or at lunch, or in a car, two of us expect to be killed by a nuclear "exchange" within the decade.

When I was born, in early 1939, the world still regarded the bombing of civilians as scandalous and monstrous, which is the point of Picasso's painting about the Fascist air attack on the Spanish village of Guernica. About the time that Hitler was defeated and Hiroshima was bombed, I started kindergarten. The year I went to college, Sputnik went up, dramatizing the potential for intercontinental ballistic missiles. Shortly after my graduation came the Cuban missile crisis, during which Jack and Bobby Kennedy had their famous chat in the Rose Garden about the fifty-fifty odds of nuclear war. In the time it took my generation to grow up, the world went from the old distinction between civilians and combatants to the wrecking of entire cities, and then to standing threats to wreck whole countries.

Many people feel quietly hopeless about this situation. One group appears to be blinded by denial, while another group would acknowledge that if we continue on the same path we will go over the cliff and yet they have no alternative to offer. Taking these two responses together, it's as if people are saying, "It will never happen and, besides, we can't stop it".... A third group, while sharing a sense of danger, just soberly assumes that we can muddle through—"After all, we've had no world war for forty years," they say, and "nobody would be so crazy...."

It's an odd feature of our age that the nuclear

system remains almost completely invisible to the ordinary citizen so long as it's not activated. People grow up, go to college, get a job, marry, travel, and do business, all without ever seeing a nuclear warhead, a missile, or even a bomber, much less a bomb test. Like a hidden cancer, the nuclear system has grown without our paying attention. Until it kills us, we may hardly notice it....

Imagine my shock when upon walking around a corner one day in Ohio I saw, at the end of a long hallway, an atomic bomb. Since I was visiting an Air Force museum,[4] I expected to see planes of all kinds, but I was not prepared to see a model of "Fat Boy," one of the bombs dropped on Japan in 1945. There it sat, like a heavy metal egg with fins. That day I happened to have rented a trailer, and I recall thinking that the bomb replica would fit in it. Yet the real thing had destroyed a city....

Many people will agree with our grim view of the current nuclear system, but within this group, only a slender fraction sees a way out. One way that we see is to appeal to the American tradition of individual action, instead of waiting for governments to alter the system that they have, in large measure, created. We are familiar, of course, with the idea that an aroused citizenry should elect leaders who embody its higher values. But we are talking about forms of action that go far beyond electoral politics, crucial as it is.

In our view, almost any government, even a democratic one, is structurally ill-adapted to transform hostility into peace. One of the primary duties of government is to identify and defend against enemies. As soon as a pair of countries begin to identify one another as enemies, as the U.S. and the Soviet Union did long ago, they generally take steps that confirm and amplify their initial fears, thus starting a familiar cycle. If a government fails to be vigilant in "threat assessment" or to procure weapons with which to threaten the enemy in return, it does not deserve to govern.

So who is left to create the conditions for peace?… We suggest that the main source of peaceful initiatives is ordinary citizens and voluntary associations or, as they are now often called, "non-governmental organizations." This is citizen summitry—the application of non-governmental energies to the highest matters of state.

Citizen diplomats don't negotiate anything with formal diplomats of the other side. They simply suggest, if only by their presence, that we could be rivals rather than enemies. The book that I brought to Moscow to distribute among contributors and others was a vision of a post-Cold-War future in which we might collaborate and certainly not threaten to make radioactive "rubble bounce"[5] in the other side's respective homelands. It did not assume that either government was effective in seeking peace; its first job was security. Peace might come in part from personal contacts: hospitality and exchange instead of threats.

The nuclear rockets and submarines were real, but the forces could be scaled down to a secure second strike capacity. In other words, each side could "absorb" a surprise attack and nonetheless "deliver" a devastating response. In this case, why would any rational leader order a strike? At the same time, a rhetoric of threats could be replaced by agreements.

This would at least be a step in the right direction.

In public opinion surveys before the start of the 1980s, a majority of U.S. voters expected a nuclear war to occur in their lifetimes. This was fatalistic but not unrealistic. As a subsequent chapter will show, an exchange nearly *did* happen. Something similar is being felt now with regard to global climate change. It's possible, but what can we do?

PRECURSORS

The citizen diplomacy activity of the 1980s did not spring from nothing. There had been efforts since the start of the Cold War, in which people without official government position sought to deal with the danger of nuclear war. Some of these efforts featured particular occupational groups, such as scientists and others (as in the Pugwash movement for a world free of nuclear weapons) and medical doctors (as in Physicians for Social Responsibility and, in the 1980s, International Physicians for the Prevention of Nuclear War). Some were mass movements in the West, such as the Committee for Nuclear Disarmament (in the U.K.) and The Committee for a SANE Nuclear Policy[6] (in the U.S.). Some were brilliant exchange efforts that brought networking to a new level (as in the Esalen Institute's program).

Professions such as physics and medicine were (and are) global, as recognized later, for example, in the organization called Doctors Without Borders. Popular movements such as CND and SANE put pressure on their governments, or at least advanced a different vision, as "dissidents" tried at great risk to do in the USSR.

I had a personal experience of this pressure during the year after college when I was given a fellowship to study at the London School of Economics. That year CND held a huge rally in Trafalgar Square not many blocks from the Prime Minister's office. I was looking for a local event to cover for a journalism competition sponsored by *TIME* magazine. After the rally I managed to talk with Bertrand Russell, the famous philosopher and activist, who had spoken to the crowd. I conducted the interview while walking briskly backwards, which wouldn't have been a problem if I had not nearly fallen off the curb into the path of a double-decker bus. I was stopped by the strong arm of Lord Russell, who was a bit amused by the eager young American and reflexively reached out, at the age of 89, to prevent a near stranger from falling.

When I went to work for Ark years later, the new element in citizen diplomacy was the exchange of people between the two superpowers, people who were not celebrities or officials and were free to imagine a viable future, without acting as negotiators.

With the best of intentions, citizen diplomats tried everything they could think of and get away with. Some, such as Esalen's program, sought out leadership networks. Others, such as Sharon Tennison's group, focused on ordinary people (and later on entrepreneurs). Into a relationship characterized by secrecy and hostility they brought openness and hospitality.

It was revolutionary to invite unofficial Soviets to the U.S. and, under the radar of the national media, receive them in hundreds of cities and have them see local business, civic, and educational life, sleep in private homes and share meals, including backyard barbecues. It is one thing abstractly to contemplate the nuclear ruin of distant cities seen only through propaganda images; another, to contemplate the horrible death of your hosts and guests.

When Alexis de Tocqueville traveled in the U.S., the basis for his famous *Democracy in America* (1835), he was struck by the many voluntary organizations he found, in which citizens, without involvement by or approval from the state, self-organized to accomplish some goal. As the Cold War threatened to become perpetual, and mutual threats came to seem natural, concerned citizens became alarmed by the system that had evolved, and sought a way out. Much of history is written by the elites that built and operated this system, on both sides, the same people who confessed they never imagined its end.

It is easy both to dismiss and to exaggerate the effect of citizen diplomacy. Some professionals in government see citizen diplomacy only as a form of "soft power," and some citizen diplomats spoke skeptically about lack of imagination in the national security elite. However, this elite was successful in managing the Cold War, if not in ending it. (For at least a quarter century.)

Citizen diplomacy would have amounted to little if at least one of the sides had not wished to change its approach. It's a complex question why Mikhail Gorbachev decided to restructure the system in which he'd risen to the top, but if he'd encountered nothing but hostility and suspicion abroad, would he have proceeded as he did? Or did he need a benign alternative toward which to move?

PUBLICITY

Once Tarcher, Inc. had published the pair of Ark books, it was our job, as co-editors, to seek favorable publicity. Don Carlson and I had the help of a professional arranger of book tours who, for a fee, would create schedules for each city, arranging interviews on TV, in newspapers, and most often on the radio. We learned about "clear channels," stations that were heard over a wide area, and about commuting hour audiences, when people with jobs were driving to work or coming home. We learned about right-wing audiences, and about local TV news shows that would put us on between a story about a rogue elephant at the zoo and an apartment house fire. We learned about book signings at stores that would pile all their copies of the books on a table, where we would offer to sign them and talk with customers.

We did over a hundred of these appearances. It was a lot of work, made easier by the generally friendly attitude of the "hosts" and reporters. We discovered that the end of the Cold War went beyond the U.S. ideological battle already being waged. Some "liberals," such as physicists who understood how dangerous nuclear weapons are, had long campaigned against them; but President Reagan also, at times, sought better relations with the USSR, as at the 1986 summit meeting in Reykjavik.

We discovered that many radio and TV producers thought they *ought* to include us on their shows, because the topic was important, but they assumed we'd be dull: peace, ugh! As Shirley MacLaine once teased us in a penetrating stage whisper in a Malibu restaurant when she asked what we were seeking, "Peace? That's the most boring thing I've ever heard! In my profession, if we tried to show peace, we'd go broke. It's tiresome." She was echoing Milton, who wrote that it was much easier to portray evil than good, but she was mainly teasing us, as we gathered from her agreement to appear at a benefit dinner.

Nonetheless, it was a useful warning, and we tried to be interesting. One game we played was that Don, the big businessman, talked about visions; and I, presumably academic, was more down-to-earth and skeptical of the extremes of citizen diplomacy hoopla. Another reason that we worked on the radio (and TV) was that we were genuinely excited about the possibility of the Cold War ending. Apart from great danger and expense, what had it brought either side? We couldn't be dismissed as fatuous peaceniks, or as people who favored the other side: obviously we weren't and we didn't.

One talk show host, just before we went live, warned us that his audience was right-wing and we were "on the hot seat." Imagine our surprise when most of the callers asked, "where have you guys been?" meaning that it was about time somebody spoke up. Scheduled for one segment of a show, during the tour we were often kept on for two or three.

Authors traditionally complain about book tours, which certainly have tedious aspects. But after one morning in a Los Angeles studio, Don said he'd reached more people in that appearance than in his entire business career, which had included talking at frequent large investor meetings. And some of the hosts were quite thoughtful to talk with, in which case we were able to focus more on them than on an invisible radio audience. We also enjoyed the variety of formats, whether right-wing listeners, housewives, commuters, academics, lovers of jazz, Spanish surnamed, top 40 lovers, whatever. On the call-in shows, very few argued that the Cold War ought to continue. It's just that almost everyone had assumed it was going to go on forever.

Probably my favorite appearance was on WGBH, in the Boston area, on a TV panel including the head of a scientists' group and also Richard Haas, later President of the Council on Foreign Relations. I had just returned from Reykjavik and Moscow. Don was right that this geographical hobnobbing gave my words a certain authority.

I argued that President Reagan seemed "out of his depth" at the summit meeting, an impression deepened when I later read the detailed notes of the negotiating sessions as kept by each side. Dr. Haas, who was then a professor at my old college, said politely that he wouldn't put it quite like that, but then, in more upholstered language, made a similar point.

I don't know what effect Don and I may have had on the millions who heard our message, but I hope it contributed to an openness to the idea of changing the relations between our country and the Soviets. In politics, perhaps the most crucial move is from denial to a feeling that some alternative deserves consideration, rather than any dream of an activist on one side going straight to the other end of the political spectrum.

And perhaps the most convincing speakers are those who acknowledge their own ambivalence or at least the counter-arguments that could be made. In other words, we tried to share our suspicion of Soviet motives and to specify what would indicate sincerity, while envisioning a big change.

Sometimes you go through a long process and it turns out to be all about one moment or one connection. In the case of the Ark books, one of which included some Soviet contributors, this moment came with a producer's decision on Soviet TV to interview one of the editors, who was visiting Moscow. I had an opportunity to make a few simple points. They knew I must be friendly because I'd included in the book some eminent Soviet scientists and writers. Here were my points:

We'd seen what the Cold War could give us, which was very little except danger and expense.

We wished prosperity and peace for the Soviet people.

A meaningful empire today was gained less by seizing land or overthrowing regimes, than by organizing an economy successfully. The Japanese, way off to the east of Moscow on tiny islands, with almost no fuel, were then out-exporting the USSR.

What if we worked together rather than at cross-purposes?

If I were doing that interview today I'd emphasize values other than consumerism, but the alternative presented then was sincere, attractive, and possible.

Even if the Ark books brought nothing but airtime in the U.S. and in the Soviet Union, they would have been worth the work. But our key ideas were also favorably reviewed in a publication read by the Soviet *nomenklatura*, or the ruling elite. I distributed about forty copies of the books in Moscow in the week following the Reykjavik summit. Apart from sales to individual readers, the books were acquired very widely by libraries in the U.S. As I said, they served as calling cards for invitations from electronic media producers in the U.S. and thus we were able to reach people who might not read a whole book, but could absorb the basic message over coffee, while doing housework, or in the car.

Ark brought me the fifteen minutes of fame of which Andy Warhol spoke, plus a career in the movies, a rather brief and glancing career. One day an Ark colleague told about his conversation with a woman who was Ted Turner's pilot. They had imagined that Turner, now that he'd bought Metro Goldwyn Mayer, might star in a movie. After desultory and scattered conversation, this colleague and Don said to me, "you're a writer, why not tie together what we've said and send Ted a treatment for a movie?" I accepted the assignment, as if it were a dare, but the evening ended without my finding a single focus.

I woke up early with an idea and quickly jotted down my first movie "treatment," which is basically the outline of a story. At the office I faxed it to the hotel in Manhattan where Turner was preparing for a live TV appearance. The next day I was told that someone in the TV studio had asked him on the air whether he'd ever thought of acting in the movies, and he said no, he hadn't, until he'd read a treatment the previous night. It was not clear that he was referring to the thing we'd sent.

The next weekend, however, Don ran into Tom Hayden, author of the Port Huron statement issued by the Students for a Democratic Society, later the husband of Jane Fonda. Hayden had asked Don whether he knew this guy Turner. Why? said Don. Well, Turner had called and asked to speak to "Jane."

Turner wanted to know whether she'd agree to read the treatment and, if she liked it, to play the female lead. From the description of the story, it was clearly our treatment. The movie never got made, but Turner and Fonda later married. This was the extent of my career in the movies, but our support for citizen diplomacy bore more fruit.

7

Meeting the Other Side

I'd planned my first trip to Moscow via Reykjavik, the capitol of the North Atlantic island nation of Iceland. The stop was intended in part to interview a leading citizen diplomat, in part to reprise my first trip to Europe long before, which was on a cheap flight to London on the Icelandic airline.

Surprised when Gorbachev and Reagan then decided to meet in Reykjavik at the time that I was scheduled to be there, I was even more surprised when many hotel reservations, including mine, were abruptly cancelled to accommodate the media and the entourages of the visiting statesmen. Adapting, I asked the University of Iceland to supply a graduate student who could assist me. Since his wife and children were going away then, this student kindly invited me to stay in his kids' room.

I spent much of the summit in the temporary CBS control room, not because of knowing anybody but just because of looking as if I might belong. The director had perhaps under-exercised and been fed a lot of junk food in the job, but he was capable and extraordinarily cool. At one point the feed from Iceland was about to go live across the U.S., but engineers in Reykjavik were waiting for a video cassette they'd use to introduce the report. An out-of-breath messenger slid into the control room just seconds before the feed went live, and jammed the cassette into a machine. The director cued the engineer and the reporter and the show went on, as if they did this every day. (They did.) Apparently unperturbed, the director took another swig of his super-sized soft drink.

Noticing that the assembled hundreds of reporters had little to do, I scheduled a media conference for the next day in a hotel ballroom, at which I would announce the publication of *Citizen Summitry*, which was scheduled for publication, by coincidence, during the Reykjavik summit meeting. I had never held a media conference, but hoped to amuse the reporters with a bit of business borrowed from an organization called Beyond War:

The speaker drops a few BBs into a metal bucket and says the clicks stand for all the bombs exploded in World War Two. Then he invites the audience to close their eyes and says he will now pour BBs representing, on the same scale, the explosive power of the nuclear weapons manufactured by the two superpowers. Of course this goes on for an agonizingly long time.

I had brought the BBs all the way from California in a transparent sealed plastic bag. Airline security was much more lax at that time, but still, I was going to a city hosting a summit meeting. I borrowed a metal ice bucket from the hotel and practiced pouring pellets, but then was informed that the leaders were unexpectedly emerging from Hofdi House, the isolated conference center. Thus the reporters rushed off and would not be able to attend my grand event. As I recall, only a few chairs were occupied, one of them by a reporter from Swedish radio who, after my truncated presentation, recorded a long interview with me.

Why the unexpected interruption? I did not find out until secret notes on the conference[1] became available, as part of the invaluable services provided by the National Security Archive at George Washington University. Apparently Gorbachev had agreed to elimination of all nuclear weapons, if Reagan would give up his anti-missile dream that critics called "star wars." I don't know whether the Soviets would have backpedaled if Reagan had said yes, but it does appear that the U.S. anti-missile scheme couldn't be made to work in a fair test, and if it had, could be easily overwhelmed by spoof warheads. The inconvenient truth about nuclear bombs is that even a small number can create terrible damage.

Reagan and Gorbachev in Moscow, 1988

Almost every day during my job at Ark, I wondered what Gorbachev was doing as a statesman. Was he seeking to fool the West, to induce it to let down its guard? Or was he in reality offering a new foreign policy? If the latter, how should our government respond? In either case, what were the domestic constraints that he and President Reagan each faced? In what ways was Gorbachev trying to reform the system at home? Had he intended the outcome of *glasnost* and *perestroika* or was he as surprised as almost everybody else? Even if he were sincere in seeking a new relationship with the West, would it last? Would our side respond? Would future leaders be adept enough to build on his initiatives?

I'm not a Sovietologist, but I did have to make some guesses at answers in order to do my work. My main guess was that Gorbachev was aware of a domestic system that was sclerotic, corrupt, and economically crippled, that he wanted to ease international pressure while he reformed this system, and that because of a highly centralized power structure he might be able to do so, or at least start the process. It would be an irony if a Soviet leader who took seriously communist ideals would wreck the party that ruled in their name. After reading a shelf of books on Gorbachev's era, I'm still not sure about his motives, his power, or his plans, but at Ark we necessarily proceeded on the basis of our best judgment.

The big issue we faced was access to Soviet people who were capable of something beyond parroting the party line. It's hard to recall now how isolated people there were, how cut off from what the rest of the world was seeing on TV or in the movies, hearing on the radio, reading in newspapers, periodicals, and books. Exit visas were hard to get. Of course, some broadcasts of the Voice of America got through the jamming, and some other, illegal channels existed, including the famous *samizdat* or underground domestic writings. It's not that Soviet citizens necessarily believed the propaganda they were fed, but they didn't have much else.

Thus, the Soviet government had set up an almost revolutionary situation by depriving their citizens of normal contact with the outside world. Just meeting an ordinary citizen of the West, or seeing a friendly visitor on TV, or reading a Western book about means of security other than mutual threats: this had a dramatic effect that would have been impossible without decades of deprivation. You could almost see people in Moscow thinking, "aren't they said to hate us?" It was almost unprecedented to hear a loyal citizen of the U.S. tell a Soviet TV interviewer, as I did, that he wished prosperity and liberty for the Soviet people.

We were amused when we first heard the popular Soviet side-of-the-mouth saying, "they pretend to pay us, and we pretend to work." Then the sadness of the situation hit us. What they were saying was they couldn't take pride in their work, and then they couldn't buy things available in many other countries and not always basics made or grown at home.

A CHALLENGE IN MOSCOW

On my first trip to Moscow I brought copies of *Citizen Summitry,* which included Soviet chapters, hoping to give the books to contributors there and to others whom I had the good fortune to meet. Whatever would be the effect of a "peace" book on the U.S. market, the volume created a good impression in Moscow, in part because of the local contributors, in part because the editors envisioned what the Soviets began to call a "normal" world, in which our two countries would be something other than enemies.

As a visitor to Moscow, I had gone shopping, not as most tourists did in a *berioska* tourist shop or at the GUM department store that stocked furs and other costly goods across from the Kremlin, but in a neighborhood store that sold chicken eggs to local shoppers. With my translator, I joined the line outside, and when we got inside saw there were three counters we had to negotiate where we'd select the eggs we wanted, pay for them, and then collect them. (When we were done, I gave the eggs away to my helper.) This was not prosperity.

Then I went to a meeting. The (American) chairwoman invited about fifty participants from both countries to discuss what they'd do together if the Cold War were ever to end, improbable as that seemed in 1986. People were reluctant to start talking. Such a discussion was unprecedented, and any imagining of collaboration might seem disloyal. While the governments had each threatened for years to destroy the other country, almost nobody had imagined normal relations. The chair said the exercise was just a form of counter-factual play, nobody would be blamed for anything said, and we'd forget everything during lunch. Then discussion slowly began. Once kindled, it became so enthusiastic that people didn't want to stop to eat.

Having studied play, I saw the power of pretending that something wasn't realistic, the power being that people began to think, "why not?" You don't extend empathy to enemies, but if you enter a pretense, and the person sitting next to you is a potential partner, or even a business competitor, the released energy can be enormous.

We made clear that we understood that the game didn't change anything outside: that the rocket forces on both sides were still gazing at their radar screens, ready to unleash the nuclear mastifs. They wouldn't watch less unceasingly because we were pretending. But as people in that Moscow room began to consider a very different world, they came alive, as the Soviet contributors to our books had. Eggs were still hard to buy, but some of us had begun imagining a different world.

TRANSPARENCY

In the course of setting up a "teleport" between the two countries, we spoke with a Soviet man we'd heard was a member of the secret police. Computer-based in a way familiar mainly to scientists then and to almost everybody now, our system would connect journalists, academics, scientists, and others who were exploring alternatives to the Cold War. To create the network, we simply leased a phone line from Moscow to Finland, and satellite time over the Atlantic to the U.S., with "nodes" at both ends.

We told the secret police official we assumed that his agency would be monitoring the messages, but whatever our views on government monitoring of private exchanges, we had nothing to hide in these messages flashing over the Iron Curtain. (It never occurred to us that our own government would ever use fear of "terrorism," despite the Bill of Rights, to grab data in the manner of a totalitarian system.)

We actually said that in a few months we'd check back with the Soviet official and ask whether, in his view, there were any improvements we could make in the system. I don't know what he and his colleagues speculated we were up to, but it must have been confusing: we were doing exactly what we said.

In short, we went as far as we could go, under the rather vague policies announced by Gorbachev: what exactly was *glasnost* or *perestroika*? In contrast with the Soviet past, these slogans gave just enough political cover for what we were doing, which had the merit of seeking only an outcome positive for both countries.

Perhaps the main value of citizen diplomacy, in that situation, was to assure reformers in the Soviet system that they might be successful in changing the relations between the countries, and suggest to politicians in the U.S. that, improbable as it might seem, a different relationship could develop.

In contrast to U.S. citizen diplomats who worked for decades with the people then called Soviets, I did little personally, apart from helping to make grants and suggesting some programs. In Moscow, I gave a Soviet TV interview emphasizing that some Americans wanted people on the other side to have happy lives. After a conversation with "the father of the Soviet space program," I did carry home some specific ideas about the maladroitness of the "star wars" proposals then current. I did talk about nuclear policy with a Soviet "commentator" who had been a key adviser to Nikita Khrushchev[2] during the Cuban missile crisis in 1962 and was still close to the top Soviet leadership.

Almost everything was fluid, waiting to be defined. Walking across Red Square at dusk with a U.S. colleague, past little cars containing police officers, I heard my companion declare, quite loudly, "this system is never going to change as long as it worships a mummy." Gesturing to Lenin's tomb, which was to Moscow what St. Peter's is to the Roman Church, he said, "the old boy should be taken out of town and given a decent burial." This was going a bit far, I felt, especially in the presence of the police cars. But many other features of Soviet life were changing. The ice was starting to melt.

Ark wanted to explore whether the Cold War was necessary and, if not, whether both sides could understand they would be better off without it. Don Carlson had made a leap that had earlier been impossible except, for example, for anti-nuclear campaigners and for peace groups (in both cases including scientists and technologists).

Troubles in the Soviet economic system, plus a war scare in 1983, the defeat in Afghanistan, and the explosion at Chernobyl in early 1986, no doubt made the Soviets less resistant than usual to changes. Gorbachev's concept of *glasnost* allowed the Soviet system to become less opaque ("a riddle wrapped in a mystery, inside an enigma," as Churchill had once said).

The fact that the right-wing held power in the U.S., which had earlier made possible the "opening" to China, also allowed Reagan to be sometimes not unwelcoming to Soviet initiatives and even to back away, as he did on Red Square in 1988, from his line about the "evil empire." It was an opportune historical moment, though perhaps neither side saw clearly how big the change would become.

If the seeds of citizen diplomacy had fallen on stony soil, to allude to a Biblical parable, the whole exercise could have been inconsequential. But in the unusual historical situation, what was still needed was a repeated gesture of friendship, a vision of something other than eternal nuclear threats. The Soviets believed their own propaganda, as did we: on the other side were monsters. The case for détente was not hard to make, in both countries, especially as facts emerged about "war scares" and plans for pre-emptive strikes.

When citizen diplomacy showed the other face of humanity, the image began to change. Hospitality, friendship, curiosity, openness: this, too, can become real. Many of those who served as citizen diplomats were not looking for paradise; they were hoping that enemies could become rivals, that nuclear war would become much less probable. Such a change would not solve many other problems; it would simply give us space to work on them.

A NUCLEAR SECRET

On a citizen diplomacy trip to Moscow in October 1986, I learned a disturbing secret about the Cuban missile crisis that shocked Robert McNamara when he first heard the Soviet secret six years later. The consequences of this secret continue to be relevant today.

During the crisis in 1962, McNamara had been U.S.

Secretary of Defense; and my Soviet source had been a close aide to Nikita Khrushchev who had sent missiles and warheads to Cuba and decided, at the climax of the crisis, to remove them. That crisis, which lasted thirteen days for the U.S. side, has been called the most dangerous moment in human history.

What the former aide told me, over coffee, was that before the climax of the crisis the Soviets had already brought to Cuba not only big missiles that could reach much of the U.S., but also, unknown to JFK and his aides, "tactical" nuclear weapons for delivery systems that could be used to repel a U.S. naval invasion of the island.

As I knew from Robert Kennedy's account (published in 1969, after the author's murder), U.S. leaders seriously considered launching an invasion of Cuba and made preparations to do so. According to Michael Dobbs in *One Minute to Midnight* (2008), arguments in favor of doing so were presented by the President's National Security Advisor McGeorge Bundy, by members of the Joint Chiefs, by Senators Russell and Fulbright, and by others.

Having been in Reykjavik on the way to Moscow during the 1986 summit meeting between President Reagan and Secretary Gorbachev, I was even more attuned than usual to the possibility of accidental nuclear war. In Reykjavik, I was no closer to high-level negotiations about the nuclear standoff than the CBS television control room, but since then, thanks in part to the Freedom of Information Act, many of the papers about the summit meeting are now available online.

After coffee with the former Khrushchev aide, it never occurred to me that U.S. intelligence had not subsequently discovered the presence in Cuba in 1962 of Soviet tactical nuclear warheads (as perhaps they did after McNamara had left the Pentagon). It seemed likely that my Soviet source was trying not to scare me, but to find a way to prevent a future miscalculation, to reduce the probability of something like the Cuban missile crisis ever happening again. I regarded the information as an example of the new and uncertain policy of *glasnost* or openness.

My modest contribution was to suggest that the former Khrushchev aide and other principals and staff on both sides could meet and share their perceptions during the crisis, and to mention some possible sponsoring organizations, mainly academic. A series of meetings did occur, including one held in Havana in 1992, at which McNamara learned about the tactical nuclear weapons.

In the Havana meeting when Castro told about the anti-invasion nukes, McNamara was so upset that he thought the translation must be bad ("I couldn't believe what I was hearing"). He asked Castro three questions: Did the Cuban leader know in 1962 about the Soviet nuclear warheads then on the island? Would he have suggested that the nukes be used against the U.S.? And if they were used, what did he think would happen to Cuba?

In the frank atmosphere of these retrospective meetings, Castro replied that he did know during the crisis that the Soviets had brought nukes to Cuba (including ninety tactical warheads, said McNamara in the documentary movie, *The Fog of War*[3]); he (Castro) had in fact suggested to Khrushchev that nuclear missiles in Cuba be fired at the U.S.; and if his advice were taken, he expected his country to be totally destroyed. Further, Castro offered his opinion that if McNamara and JFK had been in a similar situation, they would have acted as he did.

In *The Fog of War*, McNamara pauses, at a loss for words, overcome by emotion, and reports that he replied to Castro,

"Mr. President, I hope to God we wouldn't have done it. Pull down the temple on our heads? My God!"

My amiable coffee in Moscow happened more than twenty-three years after the missile crisis, so any secrets from that episode were no longer operational but archival in nature. (Our conversation occurred about as long after that crisis in 1962 as the crisis itself came after the start of World War Two, or as Stalin called it, the Great Patriotic War). Nonetheless, the lesson about the rich possibilities of miscalculation remains relevant now.

Why was McNamara so upset? Until that meeting in 1992, he had been unaware that the Soviets already had tactical nuclear warheads stationed in Cuba (though U.S. intelligence had discovered delivery systems for tactical warheads). He was upset because, as I've said, one option seriously considered by the President's special "executive committee" was an invasion of Cuba. Preparations were being made. When the crisis was settled, the planned invasion was only a couple of days away.

Dean Acheson, who had been a distinguished Secretary of State under Truman and who as an elder was invited into U.S. deliberations during the Cuban missile crisis, called the outcome "pure dumb luck." But if JFK had followed Acheson's advice, and that of several members of his inner circle, top military leaders, Senators, and others—to attack as many of the known missiles as possible and then to invade the island—and if the Soviets had fired even some of the tactical nuclear weapons they had (including one aimed at the Guantanamo base), where would a nuclear exchange have stopped?

Luck was also invoked by McNamara, who favored the blockade or "quarantine" adopted by JFK, and who like Acheson did not then know about the Soviet tactical nukes. In *The Fog of War*, slashing his hand at the camera, McNamara says, "it was luck [pause] that prevented nuclear war." Holding his index finger a quarter inch from his thumb, he added, "We came that close."

The point for today is that, when nuclear weapons are involved, we are one step away from irreparable consequences. A friend of mine defines humans as "quasi-domesticated primates with power tools." As Jonathan Schell warned us in *The Fate of the Earth* as long ago as 1982, the tools now include a collection of nuclear missiles capable of casting into the shadows even World War Two and the events of those years.

A mythology grew up about JFK's crisp performance as a crisis manager. The dominant lesson learned by the "best and brightest" was that in a crisis, you should show some restraint: don't pull down the temple (in McNamara's phrase) or tug on the ends of a rope in which the knot of war has been tied (Khrushchev's). Instead, consider your options carefully and offer the other side an acceptable deal.

At the end of the Cuban missile crisis, the way out was a U.S. initiative, an agreement under which the Soviet missiles would be swiftly removed from Cuba, in return for a U.S. promise not to invade that island and a secret and oral promise that U.S. would withdraw missiles from Turkey in four to five months. Since the latter missiles were old-fashioned and vulnerable anyway, the U.S. considered that it had prevailed. As McNamara reported in *The Fog of War*, he took the Joint Chiefs of Staff to the White House where JFK told them our side had won (but they were to be tactful and not claim victory).

Perhaps if JFK had not allowed the prior Bay of Pigs invasion to be launched and then aborted, and if he had not permitted Khrushchev to treat him roughly at the 1961

Vienna summit, Khrushchev might have hesitated ever to send nuclear weapons to Cuba. In that case, there would have been no crisis to manage.

A nuclear war represented by what Khrushchev called a "knot" would have meant destruction for both superpowers (and for places where they had military forces), and probably "nuclear winter" as well. According to McNamara, it was barely untied, that knot.

Apart from the necessity to have cool heads during a crisis or to pick the option that works, what is the lesson of McNamara holding his fingers barely apart and saying, "we came that close" to nuclear war? Will good "crisis management" and "luck" be enough in the long run?

In financial analysis, "black swan" has become a popular metaphor for dangers that are very high in negative consequences, even if they seem vanishingly low in probability. For example, in terms of the behavior of big banks, the economic crisis of 2008 (and beyond); in terms of nuclear power, Chernobyl; in terms of storms, the effects of Katrina; in terms of deep sea drilling, the BP geyser in the gulf; in terms of earthquake, the Fukushima nuclear power plants; or in terms of rocketry, Challenger (which had happened in 1986, the year when I first visited Moscow). These crises share a theme: the very low estimated probability of their happening. Obviously, they did happen. But has this lesson been learned? In the documentary about him, McNamara remarks that he knew of three situations that nearly ended in a nuclear exchange.

Since the years after 1991, the U.S. has preened itself as the sole remaining superpower, but the world is still full of nuclear weapons, including warheads in the hands of enemies of each other (India, Pakistan), a potential rival of ours (China), what is called a rogue state (North Korea), plus the core of the former USSR (Russia), European allies of ours (France, Great Britain), and Middle East states (Israel and, perhaps in the near future, Iran). Apart from their existence, at least some of these warheads and many nuclear materials are ill-guarded and, in any case, subject to the kind of secrets and miscalculation that occurred in the Cuban missile crisis.

THE WALL

According to Don's original proposal to me, Ark's involvement in helping to end the Cold War was scheduled to end in 1989. It was a coincidence that the Berlin Wall was breached in the same year, providing a theatrical conclusion for our work.

That urban barrier book-ended much of my adult life. During a post-college fellowship when I was based in London, I traveled east in autumn 1961 to meet a friend who was marrying a Berlin woman. We volunteered to bring some heart medicine to some of her relatives in the eastern zone (or Ost Sektor, as it was locally called).

I gather we were some of the first westerners through the wall at Checkpoint Charlie, where tanks of the two sides had faced off. Slipping our passports through a slot in a wall, we wondered whether we'd ever see them again, but no problem: soon we were walking past the site of Hitler's bunker, on our way to a Marxist bookshop, where we learned that Stalin had written (or at least signed) an entire book on the linguistics problem. The range of titles was drastically more limited than in our college bookstores, consisting mainly of works by Marx, Engels, and dictators who professed to be enacting their ideas.

After that day, I did not see the Wall again on my visit until wandering down Bernauerstrasse and finding two boys at play across from a former butcher shop *(fleischerei)* in a building where the windows had been replaced by bricks. It was dusk. The wall of concrete blocks was almost beautiful, hastily constructed not with geometric precision but sloping lazily over the curb of a cross street. I was starting into a callow aesthetic appreciation when I glanced upward and saw an East German border guard pointing an automatic weapon in my direction.

As we confirmed later, the Wall also came up in the U.S. deliberations during the Cuban missile crisis. Was the Wall erected hastily in 1961 the least-bad outcome? For the East it solved the problem of people fleeing to the Western part of the city and, for the West, served as a symbol of the failure of East Germany. In 1962 would the Soviets nonetheless use the missile crisis as an excuse to block Western access to Berlin?

There the Wall stood for twenty-eight years, part of a metaphorical "iron curtain," actually a barrier of cement (and a mine field), or as I saw on a West German torchlight-parade sign, Wall of Shame and Barbed Wire[4] *(Schandmauer und Stacheldraht).*

JFK showed his solidarity by proclaiming *"Ich bin ein Berliner,"* a noun which in local idiom refers to a favorite pastry, but the crowd understood what he meant. Not to be upstaged, Reagan later challenged Gorbachev to "tear down this wall." With the Soviet army staying in its barracks, the demolition was accomplished in 1989 by exultant Berliners. Soon the wall existed only in the form of rubble, thousands of souvenir chunks, and sections left standing as a sort of memorial.

Hardened enemies had become rivals. After the Cuban missile crisis, JFK privately told his administration to avoid gloating. After the breakup of the Soviet Union, top U.S. leaders allowed, even encouraged, the rise of U.S. triumphalism, as if the failure of the USSR proved the rightness of the surviving economic system.

IMPOSSIBLE IDEAS

Citizen diplomacy attracted many kinds of folks. Some Westerners only sought to talk with ordinary Soviet people. Some focused on leaders, and created a network of associations with well-placed people in the Soviet system, eventually including top leaders. Some hosted visitors in their homes in the U.S. Almost all of them took on tasks that seemed impossible, as in the case of Sharon Tennison,[5] another in the list of unsung heroes I had the good fortune to encounter.

Sharon was a nurse in San Francisco when she was asked by a member of Physicians for Social Responsibility to talk to a local group about the Cold War. She realized she knew very little about the USSR. Her way of repairing this common ignorance was to walk into the Soviet consulate on Green Street and ask about making a trip to Moscow. Once she had applied for her visa, she told friends, some of whom volunteered to join her. Soon she created an organization, the Center for US-USSR Initiatives (CUUI), later known as the Center for Citizen Initiatives.

At the time we at Ark were looking for people who didn't care that their hope would be called impossible, who didn't wait for a grant to get started, and who were adventurous, ingenious, and persistent. When Sharon and I met for breakfast, she was soon leaving for another trip to Moscow. As she tells in her book, *The Power of Impossible Ideas*, "We had barely sat down for brunch at Mama's Café in Oakland when Craig threw out a question, 'what is the most effective action that CUUI could organize [in the] next year to ease tensions between the two superpowers?' Stunned at the question and guessing that money was probably behind it, my mind reeled." Recovering quickly over our scrambled eggs, Sharon imagined an exchange program "of Soviet citizens coming to the U.S. to meet American citizens in hundreds of cities and towns."

At this time, such an exchange program was wholly unprecedented. I saw my job at Ark as getting people into trouble such that, as they proceeded, they might do something wonderful. With a straight face, I suggested that she tell her contacts in Moscow that we wanted to invite 500 Soviet "unofficials" to visit the U.S. We imagined each small group going to several cities, staying in private homes, and seeing schools, small businesses, the city council, backyard barbecues, whatever.

Sharon and I started writing on paper napkins. As she explains in her book, "The Soviets would be non-party people selected by CUUI, and they would show American citizens that really good, genuine people live in the other superpower." Aeroflot would be asked to let these citizen diplomats fly free in otherwise empty seats on scheduled flights to and from the U.S.

Organizers here would be found more in the Rotary clubs than on the peacenik fringe. The program would be called "Soviets, Meet Middle America." At social occasions, the Soviets would be introduced by Representatives, Mayors, or other high political figures. We'd focus publicity not on the national media but on local papers and local radio and TV stations.

We asked for Soviet people who were not government officials, but were teachers, psychologists, scientists, and other folks who had enough English to communicate. We knew that the secret police would probably infiltrate some groups, but figured these people needed to be educated, too. Ark would come up with a grant to cover coordination of the program by Sharon's organization.

Of course we both knew this program might never happen. As Sharon writes in her memoir, "My overwhelming concern was how to find a crack in the Soviet concrete to make this vision possible." In one sense, the concrete took the form of the necessary exit visas being available only to party members, and only to a few of those.

However, being persistent and ingenious, Sharon found that Gorbachev had chosen a young man as "his 'point person' for exit visas and other never-before-tried, radical experiments." His name was Gennady Alferenko, a dance impresario who had worked outside the system, living as he did on the edge, in far-away Novosibirsk. But to whom should he grant the much-sought-after exit visas? Gennady and Sharon formed a partnership.

The result was "Soviets, Meet Middle America," which carefully sought no national publicity but was covered extensively by local media in hundreds of U.S. cities. By design, the visitors were often introduced by local politicians, including members of Congress. Thus, hundreds in the U.S. political sector had mingled at barbecues or sat in living rooms with Soviet visitors. Being affable, these American politicians soon had Soviet friends to talk about, no longer just abstractions.

If Sharon had worked only until the fall of the Berlin Wall in 1989, she would have made a historic contribution in a form that she helped to develop. But she didn't stop. Teaming up with Rotary International, she continued until the present (I'm writing in 2016). One of the projects was to develop a network of small businesspeople throughout Russia. The people would visit the U.S. and observe the operation of the kind of business they wanted to start, and back home they'd get support and advice from other members of the program.

Sharon calls her book *The Power of Impossible Ideas*. She wasn't sure that many of her projects would work, but she knew they were necessary and took the risk. The risk was no smaller than that taken by many business leaders who claim they wouldn't be motivated unless they stood a chance of deriving great wealth. Apparently, other motivations can lead to great ends.

I could have written about many other citizen diplomats, such as, among Ark's other grantees, the Esalen Institute's Soviet-American Exchange Program or World Without War. Many people took part, a tribute to the volunteer spirit and to freedoms guaranteed in our Bill of Rights.

WHY NOT?

Various U.S. administrations have sought to do "public diplomacy," but however effective this has been, it is not the same as what Ark sponsored. Public diplomacy is an official effort to show the attractive sides of a country, to keep the focus on liberty (as we see it) or on blue jeans and popular music, rather than on military occupation or bases or the offer of loans (indebtedness). Citizen diplomacy is about changing our policy from an assertion of power to a *modus vivendi*, a way of living together as equals.

Citizen diplomacy starts with respect and empathy. You don't assume you are better; you assume the other culture is different and show curiosity about it. In his speech at American University,[6] JFK imagined World War Two as the Soviets experienced it, saying that if a comparable invasion had happened in the U.S. we would have been occupied all the way from the eastern seaboard to the suburbs of Chicago. When I first visited in Moscow twenty-three years after this speech, it was still being cited. On the road from the airport into the city was a monument showing where

Hitler's Wehrmacht was stopped.

Far from being an adjunct to professional international relations, citizen diplomacy proposed a path that was not pioneered by the pros, and was to some extent fought by some of them or ridiculed. Citizen diplomacy was explicitly critical of the national security elite, not because its members didn't do their job skillfully and sincerely, but because they showed few signs of seeing beyond the confines of their job. As Eisenhower said, out of first-hand experience, governments are much better at fighting wars than making peace.

The national security elite knew how to run the Cold War, and barring a miscalculation, could prevent any Soviet nuclear adventuring by plausibly threatening retaliation ("make the rubble bounce from Riga to Vladivostok"). What they didn't necessarily know how to do was to end the Cold War.

The Soviet Union under Gorbachev was made for citizen diplomacy. While there were restrictions on some travel, the country was physically safe, safer than some U.S. cities. Moscow or St. Petersburg were hardly further from the U.S. than destinations in Western Europe frequented by millions of travelers. Soviet citizens were starved for outside contact, after years of no exit visas and zapping of foreign broadcasts. Aeroflot was willing, in certain cases, to give away empty seats on flights to the U.S. Citizen diplomats had access to some Soviet mass media, in part because of our rarity. Soviet innovators there were looking for foreign models, if not with the systematic avidity of Japanese travelers, then with more than casual attention to Spanish or Scandinavian social democracy, for example.

The national security elite may feel, "Don't they understand? Nuclear weapons have kept the peace, sort of, at least between the superpowers, for decades. Of course there's a risk. With weapons there always is. But it was tolerable. After all," they might say in a self-satisfied way, "we've never had a nuclear exchange, despite some scares."

The opposition replies: "Some events are so bad they are intolerable, including the destruction of the northern hemisphere by nuclear weapons. There have been several near-misses, with the Kennedy brothers once telling each other at dusk during the Cuban missile crisis that while death wasn't so terrible for adults, think of the kids who never will have a chance to live. The deterrence system depends on a rationality on which we can't rely."

It's a facile ideological analysis to say that the U.S. spent the USSR into the ground and they had no choice but to surrender. It's equally silly to say once we extended the hand of friendship the Cold War was inevitably over, because the other side never wanted it anyway. It's perhaps less silly to say a process of reciprocity began, with suspicion on both sides, but also a motive to explore the possibilities. The U.S. did not "win" the Cold War; that war was allowed to lapse. For a long while, in any case, we found another way to relate.

Contact is most valuable not when it merely displays the virtues of one side, as "public diplomacy" does, but when it asks, "why not peace?" In a phrase often on the lips of citizen diplomats, "when the people lead, the leaders will follow."

An Invitation

8

Openness to Experience

The value of my particular story centers mainly on an attitude toward new things, or what psychologists call "openness to experience." Another way to think about this is: willingness to keep learning. When Nevitt Sanford and I gathered his papers about life-long education, we chose the title *Learning After College*.[1] I don't think of myself as a virtuoso of learning, but I had the good fortune to have mentors and partners who were.

Many people aren't very attracted to the activity of learning. Perhaps they were humiliated in school, or made to feel stupid. Perhaps they were happy to get through one adolescence, and are not eager to repeat the practice of not knowing but feeling you have to pretend that you do.

Perhaps their parents reinforced them more for knowing, than for learning. If you think about it, the guiding light of the educational enterprise is tests of knowledge, the fruit of learning. Our attention is focused on the fruit, not on the tree that intricately creates it and without which it wouldn't exist. A wise mentor might notice and support the process of learning, but it's not seen on a multiple-choice test.[2]

As we observed at the William James Center for Adult

Development, it's often not rewarded, the process of being willing to try something new, to find a mentor, to make mistakes quickly and learn from them, to focus less on knowing facts than on being able to find them and to act even when the situation isn't clear. Some people see themselves as a repository of actionable conclusions; others, more as creatures of curiosity.

This emphasis on curiosity has implications for parenting, for schooling, for the management of people, for our own practice of life-long learning. It is fine to paint a picture of success, but learning includes failures. How do we respond to failures, especially in a culture that rewards the appearance of continual success?

Much success in business or any other enterprise cannot be fairly described without invoking luck. Out of ten people with an ingenious idea for a computer application, say that one person makes a fortune, the others do okay, get by, or fade away. Was the successful person the best? Sometimes yes, sometimes no. If we worship success, the reasoning becomes circular. But "luck" doesn't fit the ideology of "free market" fundamentalism.

PROMOTING CREATIVITY

How would you go about, as a parent, a teacher, a manager, a colleague, encouraging the practice of creativity? My wife is a painter and I have heard much discussion of "talent." Some people come to her classes and start by declaring, "I'm not creative." What does that even mean? I'm afraid to try? I could never do your kind of art? I'm irremediably conventional?

The founder of the art center in our town rues the way many people identify creativity only with the so-called fine arts. By her definition, there is an opportunity for creativity not only in the studio, but, for example, in the nursery, the classroom, in the office or other workplace. Again, this sounds like a generous way of thinking. But as a good artist knows, doing something new involves repeated failure, or as it's more politely called, substantial trial and error. Not always, but often. Einstein said that if an idea does not seem absurd at first, it can't be important.

You need to have support for this process. The pressure to be right is the enemy of bold experiment, and of fooling around. As I explained in Chapter 2, a coaching client taught me that the fool is not necessarily an idiot (or a Shakespearean teller of truth through humor). As in the Tarot, the fool might be seen as what Buddhists call "beginner's mind."[3] The visual image suggests a person who starts things, some of which work.

What would it be like to live in a society where people are admired not for being "winners" but for being "learners"? Of course this cuts against our natural admiration for strong people who can pile up assets. Like many human values, the process of learning must be taught; it's no more "natural" than a Rembrandt or van Gogh. Making early love, going off to college, becoming a first-time parent, negotiating the world of work, these are common experiences of awkwardness, of not knowing quite what to do.

One reason that I required a collapse of my life was that success had come easy. When I was starting senior year in high school, my father said that I should research colleges and decide where I wanted to apply; he'd take me for interviews; he'd pay the expenses. I didn't know anything of colleges. I didn't have a tutor for the college boards. There was no advanced placement. The admissions interviewer at the college that I eventually attended declared that I was "a diamond in the rough." He was correct about the "rough" part. It all felt gratuitous, as did subsequent delights.

However, I think what made it possible was a message from my parents that life was about adventure, not about relentlessly winning. My brother was trained as an economist and early computer programmer, but became a world champion hot air balloon pilot, set records, and made possible the first round-the-world balloon flight.[4] At the age when other guys are retiring, he took up paragliding. The older of our two sisters was one of the first women to earn a doctorate in hard science at her university, the first foreigner to head a Japanese school, a successful transpacific exchange executive, and a teacher in an intensive process about family of origin. She wrote *Journey Into Love* and *Honoring Missed Motherhood*.[5] Our other sister was a student of Chinese, a fabric artist illustrated in books, and during most of her life, a teacher in the same process as her sister. My point here is not their particular achievements, but their adventurousness.

SOME PRACTICAL LESSONS

Let's get practical. What are some lessons I think I've learned from my own experience at enlarging my comfort zone and from the wisdom of people described in this book and from that of other friends?

Here are a few:

Seek mentors among experts in the area into which you hope to move. Many people love to share their wisdom, especially if you pay close attention. This doesn't mean always agreeing, but it does mean engaging.

If possible, tell people close to you what you want to do, even if they start by thinking the idea is a little weird.

Consider keeping part of what you've done before, especially if it's a source of income and it doesn't interfere with your new direction.

With part of your energy and attention, try something well outside your accustomed area. If you specialize in verbal language, try a visual art. If you are gregarious, try meditating. If you're known for precision, try cutting loose.

Set goals, and when you reach them, or fall short, reconsider. An experiment in which you don't find what you sought is not necessarily unsuccessful. And you might be surprised.

Read stories of other people who have set out to enlarge their comfort zones. This book focuses sharply on one example, including people the author encountered and admired. Add others. Ask friends and listen.

Put emphasis more on learning, less on already knowing. This is hard, because our society teaches the opposite, in many ways. There is a vulnerability in doing something other than what has been the basis of your identity, your social value, your claim to be loved. But many of the wonderful things of life happen when you are vulnerable.

Take walks, sit in the woods, do nothing.

The rest of the time, set challenges for yourself. You don't have to tell anyone else, but do when you can find support or other useful feedback.

No need to wait until retirement to enter the volunteer world. Easy to say, but how to find the time? You have a job (if you're lucky), perhaps a spouse and a family, there's the TV to keep up with, chores. But make it a priority to volunteer, perhaps to assist others. This will not help you get more stuff, but it will show you more of the world. Volunteers get to learn new skills. They don't need a resume. The directors of organizations are happy to welcome them. In a small city in Oregon, I have friends volunteering in food banks, restorative justice, a peace house, a shelter for women, community access TV, education for seniors, an "abundance swap," and so forth.

Get out more. A diet of only work, family, and TV cheats us of the rich buffet that's all around us. We become obsessive parents, unimaginative observers.

In a consumerist society, it may seem a heresy, but we don't have to spend all the money our salary provides. We can choose to live on less, and save for a period of exploration. This is easiest to do before you and perhaps others are accustomed to a certain "lifestyle."

Think of something you gave up or haven't yet developed, something you "always wanted to do." Imagine being on your deathbed: what regrets would you have? Then would be too late to act. Can you try it now?[6]

APPENDIX

Scenarios

As the Cold War faded away (after lasting from, say, the late forties to the late eighties), we did not expect to be ushered into a land of milk and honey. The system of mutual nuclear threats had overshadowed other troubles. Now these other troubles would come to the fore.

I was given a privileged seat to learn about challenges and alternatives after the Cold War had lapsed. In 1992, the Elmwood Institute[1] in the San Francisco Bay Area asked me to edit its newsletter. I was a "peer" of the institute (which just meant a member). This editorial work was a job that needed to be done; and with my experience I could do it. As a volunteer I thus discovered a new world, as I had done many times with clients as a book creation coach.

Located in the Bay Area but global in its concerns, the Elmwood Institute had been started by Fritjof Capra, author of *The Tao of Physics*. It was an honor to be invited to join this organization: I admired members of whom I'd heard, including many of the foremost social observers of our era.

Friends who were peers included Chellis Glendinning, who had already written *Waking Up in the Nuclear Age* (1987) and *When Technology Wounds* (1990). I soon met other friends in Elmwood, including Ernest (Chick) Callenbach,[2] author of *Ecotopia*. With that kind of talent among readers of the

Elmwood publication, director Zenobia Barlow and I asked, why continue to restrict ourselves to a newsletter? Why not convert it into a journal? I served as founding editor for a year, in 1992-93, to get the journal started. We called it *Elmwood Quarterly*.[3]

This was an extraordinary opportunity. The circulation was limited, but the recipients included many authors, teachers, workshop leaders, and political activists. Ideas expressed in *Elmwood Quarterly* thus had a wide circulation and long life.

In 1992 we did special issues on "redefining wealth," on "thinking about population," on "eco-literacy," and on "deep ecology": in all over 100 large pages. The issue on population reported on an international conference sponsored by the Institute and organized by Chick Callenbach. The issue on deep ecology was inspired by the work of the Norwegian Arne Naess, a pioneer in the field.

Unfortunately, many of the *Elmwood Quarterly* articles would still be fresh and timely now. (One was recently republished on the website called Resilience.com, sponsored by the Post-Carbon Institute.) This is both a tribute to the contributors and a judgment on the failure of recent mainstream journalism or, in cases where journalists have treated a subject seriously, on the denial practiced almost unconsciously by many readers.[4]

Take the inaugural issue on redefining wealth. In a consumer society, we are taught by advertising and peer pressure to define success mainly in terms of money and ability to buy stuff. This assumption is rarely even stated, seeming as natural as vehicles in the street. What other values could there be? Well, people value the family, certainly the nuclear family, the house in which it dwells, the car that transports members of it. "People of faith" value their religious practice and place. But the main goal in the U.S., to avoid being "a loser," is economic success (and the ability wisely to spend money, and in some cases invest it).

We asked the simple question, what other values could be primary? Contributors used terms such as "sustainability" and "ecology," terms now so familiar they have been hijacked by slippery corporate advertising (also called "greenwashing"). We talked about techno-addiction and alternatives to the metric of "gross domestic product"(GDP).

In 2012 the U.N. sponsored a conference on using happiness as a measure of national well-being, instead of depending only or mainly on GDP. In 1992, the *Elmwood Quarterly* was publishing Helena Norberg-Hodge on "surprising lessons about wealth we can learn from a Himalayan people." One lesson from her years in Ladakh? What counts is happiness. (Other countries that rank high in happiness include the social democracies of northern Europe.)

As editor, I had the opportunity to act as rapporteur for the population conference. I also interviewed Satish Kumar, founder of the British magazine *The Ecologist* and of Schumacher College in the U.K.; wrote on social inventors in three countries (including the founder of "The Natural Step" in Sweden); reviewed a BBC documentary on the elusive Kogi tribe in Columbia; and critiqued a *Los Angeles Times* article on writers carelessly dismissed as "Neo-Luddites" (some of whom were Elmwood peers).

In their observations and suggestions, the Institute's peers did not just make some lucky guesses. Their ideas came from coherent views of society and the desire to find alternatives to some of society's negative aspects. Their job was not to celebrate the achievements of rich countries, which are many, but to meet as best they could the challenge of the global thinker. That challenge is to ask how the population of Earth can reach its highest ideals (or as people said at the time, its potential).

While working for the Elmwood Institute, I was asked, as noted above, to report on a major conference about population. After the report was published as a special issue of *Elmwood Quarterly,* I was doing the usual publicity, which included a live radio interview during the commuting hour. In trying to illustrate the scale of population growth, I launched on a spontaneous parable of which I hadn't thought before and didn't know the exact punch-line.

Imagine, I said, that Earth's intelligence agencies receive the following radio message: "We have learned that our distant planet is going to explode in twenty years and we have decided to approach you about sending our inhabitants to Earth, where they would arrive gradually, respect your customs, learn your languages, work hard, pay taxes, and seek to assimilate."

What would be the response? I thought that the stunned leaders might recover enough to ask, "Well, this is quite a surprise but how many emigrants do you want to send each year?" The answer would come back, "XX million." I thought Earth's leaders would gasp and regard this as one of the biggest crises in human history.

Of course, the figure I gave was the net number of additional mouths on the earth each year because of global population growth, based on the number of human babies, less deaths. Like aliens, the new-borns would be unsocialized, and unlike well-intentioned alien adults, wholly dependent.

But a fast growing population is only one of the many situations with which we aren't dealing. Many of us get appeals for funds from groups promising to respond to climate change, species extinction, the financial crisis, and more.

One of the attractive features of the American mythos is an emphasis on optimism. We're a can-do people. In 1992 I assumed that we'd recognize the problems, call on our ingenuity, and act.

THREE FUTURES

As some companies, government agencies, and non-profits have found, it's helpful, even when you can't predict, to imagine and articulate some possible scenarios. The future, as usual, can unfold in many ways. Meanwhile, here are three scenarios, each of them surely wrong to some degree if taken as a prediction, but instructive: the best we can do.

Back to normal: The recession ends as economic growth returns. Jobs appear. The cost of unemployment benefits drops because people are working. With more income, people buy. World trade increases. The price of energy, influenced by new supplies, falls in real terms. Profits grow. Tax receipts from individuals and firms go up. The stock market rises. The purchasing power of the dollar is largely sustained. Consumers are able once again not only to buy more but also to feel more financially secure for the long term. Almost everybody is happy. A certain period starting in 2008 is marked on charts as a recession, after which normal prosperity returns. In short, the "downturn" was nothing worse than the familiar low point of the business cycle. What went down, then goes up. The national debt remains but even big increases feel normal. This has happened before; a recession is painful while it lasts, but it's followed by renewed prosperity.

Probably most people expect us to get "back to normal,"

but other observers don't. They see the potential for hidden changes to cause trouble, even the collapse of industrial civilization, even "near-term human extinction." Now let's consider this dismal scenario. As painful as this would be, it's useful to consider the possibility.

Collapse: According to "peak oil" analysts, the price of energy is eventually going to increase, as easy oil and other resources are replaced by energy and other resources that are harder to obtain and thus more costly. Since much of our economy is based on energy, recession continues or returns (and perhaps becomes what is called a depression). Jobs do not return from abroad, where labor is much cheaper. On the contrary, jobs in rich countries are replaced not only by production abroad, but also by the increasing use of robots. The data on unemployment rates continue to be fiddled with, based as they are on many definitions, but real unemployment rises; and some people hold jobs that are below their skills. People feel poorer because they are: some lose jobs, and everyone is affected as the purchasing power of income declines. Housing prices are sluggish as banks keep putting foreclosed properties on the market. "The greatest country in the world" finally acknowledges that it has lost its eminence in category after category, including health statistics and educational achievement. The U.S. tries to compensate for its relative decline by exercise of military power but, as in Afghanistan and Iraq, cannot prevail even at great expense. Voters realize too late that price inflation is the cruelest tax of all, especially because it's silently imposed. Meanwhile, climate change becomes undeniable, as some farm regions suffer drought and others suffer damage from flooding and severe storms. Food prices soar.

These are two scenarios at opposite extremes of optimism

and pessimism. The first is simply assumed by most of us; the second scenario is, for many people, almost unthinkable. Economic growth is like our civic religion. We depend on it as the source of our individual prosperity. Without growth, we might question the gross inequality characteristic of our economic system. Without growth, we'd no longer be the envy of the world, which, whatever attitude it has toward "our freedoms," surely admires our wealth. Without growth, how could we maintain the "American dream," as long as it's defined mainly in terms of children being better off economically than their parents?

Collapse would violate everything we have known, and thus seems improbable. As social psychologists put it, we have a bias toward normality. An uncomfortable number of analysts do argue that our system is challenged in several ways: by climate change, by peak oil, by eventual resource scarcity, by population pressures, by financial collapse based on fraud, a casino mentality, and control of government by people it's meant to regulate. They argue that our present financial system, while apparently dynamic, would lead to collapse. The alternative is not "government," at least not the present version. In fact, they'd observe that the government has been captured for most purposes by corporations.

Now, among the many scenarios we could imagine, let's consider a third.

A new system that succeeds: We start not with an ideology specifying what's allegedly right, but with design criteria, with what we want. That is, we start not with a method that may or may not have worked in the past and is familiar, but with our present goals. Designers who don't yet know how to accomplish something often start with a list of what the device or system must accomplish. For example, a lighting fixture must emit so many lumens, cost no more than a certain amount, and require maintenance no more than every so often. A list of criteria can suggest ideas and meanwhile allows the fast elimination of ideas that don't meet the goals. They help us to fail quickly, and then perhaps to succeed, sometimes in unfamiliar ways.

As described in this book, my experience of venturing into unfamiliar worlds was voluntary. I didn't have to accept any given client, and could have extracted myself from a job if it were unsatisfactory. However, the great merit of accepting a challenge was the lag it introduced into any rejection on my part. I wanted things to succeed, and therefore put up with a certain period of turbulence.

In the future, in case of the scenario of "collapse" sketched above, we wouldn't have the option of backing out. But we can meanwhile act as if we could do better, could even, in theory, evolve a system appropriate to new conditions. I wonder whether the challenge is any greater than what the Founding Fathers faced when declaring independence and then creating a federal constitution.

For example, in no particular order, let's say we want an economic system that (a) sharply cuts harmful pollution, especially the emission of greenhouse gases, (b) allocates capital to enterprises that are socially useful, (c) inculcates an ethic of "enoughness" rather than of having as much as possible, (d) encourages innovation, (e) provides everybody with the necessary minimum of income, (f) keeps inequality in a reasonable band, and (g) is sustainable in the long term. To be perfectly clear, our criteria would probably rule out a system that pollutes wildly, consumes resources including energy as fast as possible, leads to gross inequality, encourages financial gambling, has periodic severe recessions, and depends on a relatively impoverished and powerless class.

We can raise sharp questions about the criteria. For example, in discussing the list above, we'd want to ask first who decides what's "socially useful"? How much inequality is necessary to motivate people to take risks? How do we keep people working if they're guaranteed support so they don't starve? We can recognize that some of the criteria make some others harder to reach, necessitating balance.

SCIENCE SAYS

In many ways, the college graduates in my generation thrived during a golden age. The country was prosperous. With some exceptions, freedoms were largely respected. We were open to the world, which yielded knowledge about other ways of life (including practices known as "spiritual"). Members of my generation were too young for the Korean War, in many cases deferred during the U.S. involvement in Vietnam, and too old to participate in the more recent big wars (in most of which our involvement ended, as in Korea and Vietnam, in stalemate or chaos at best, even when a particular dictator was overthrown).

True, there were downsides, too, rather severe ones. Nuclear weaponry was hailed as making it unnecessary to invade Japan in 1945, but before long the U.S. was vulnerable to a Soviet nuclear attack. The year before I started high school the Soviets exploded an H-bomb, and the year I started college they put up Sputnik, using rockets that could be used to "deliver" nuclear weapons to North America. I was starting graduate school when the Cuban missile crisis brought us close to a nuclear "exchange." Of course it would have been stupid for the Soviets to attack, to the extent that the U.S. had a "secure second strike capacity," but if you removed all the stupid events from history, the story would be much easier to master.

So conditions were not ideal back then. It's true that the hydrogen bomb never exploded except in tests, but as in a Beckett play, some of us were apprehensive; we felt unsafe, a feeling that did not become widespread in the U.S. until decades later when terrorists attacked a few symbolic buildings in New York and Washington. A relatively tiny version of what had long been extremely dangerous, became even more vivid than a video game, cell phone app, or action movie.

We humans are not very good at either foreseeing the future or at listening to scientific evidence (as compared with events that we can see without instruments). The Axis challenge was obvious well before 1941, but it took the attack on Pearl Harbor to demonstrate the threat in a way, and to a degree, that mobilized this country.

The human disinclination to believe unwelcome scientific evidence, though understandable, is stunning. As in the case of cigarette smoking, doubt about any ill effects was magnified and sustained by economic interests until the evidence became overwhelming. Certainty is comfortable, but the problem is, in the case of climate change it would then be too late.

I would be delighted if I could be convinced, by the weight of scientific evidence, that global warming is not happening, not dangerous, and not caused in part by human emissions. But to regard it as a "hoax," as at least one Senator does, could itself be an extremely costly misjudgment. The issue now is whether we can avoid not some global warming and all the side effects, but even worse warming than is already, so far as we know, unavoidable.

The situation is peculiar in several ways:

Unlike the attack on Pearl Harbor, the evidence on global warming is not obvious to all lay people. The evidence is found not in huge headlines or on mainstream TV but in obscure scientific papers. Yes, the conclusions come from many fields, but most of us are experts in none of them.

Because of a temporal gap before effects become obvious, the damage to our civilization and to human life will have been assured before the danger becomes clear to the layperson, and then the effects will last for centuries.

According to Nicholas Stern of the London School of Economics, author of an authoritative report on climate change, the cost of changing our economic system might be a small percentage of GDP, but any adequate change would have to occur soon, not in the indefinite future, and would require a different economic structure than we have. It's not clear how our system could honor true sustainability, which means observing limits.

Even if our own domestic system could change, it's hard to see in advance how we could get the rest of the world to go along, especially the part of the world that is fast "developing" (but is still, in per capita terms, poor).

New challenges are often beyond the capabilities of a system, in part because the old system, the one that has been discredited by events, fights to keep its power, even as it fails even to recognize new conditions, and thus it may cause desperate problems.

We humans are quite good at meeting various threats to our survival, threats that are obvious to lay people; but other kinds of threats, not so much. Given the very slow pace of physical evolution, our new powers are mostly cultural, which is our only way of keeping up with the new phenomena enabled by what? By other aspects of cultural evolution. In other words, we invent nuclear weapons, then hustle to assure they aren't used, or given the near-accidents, should hustle. We invent ways to get fossil fuels out of the Earth and burn them, then discover the effects of greenhouse gases. Meanwhile we have an industrial revolution and develop a dependence on its benefits, build a pattern of life based upon it: the way we get around, for example, or the way we grow and distribute food, or the way we heat and cool buildings, or the way we make things.

In the early 1990s, we had reason to hope. In 1985 scientists were astonished to discover a "hole" in the protective layer of ozone around the earth. Because of local conditions, this hole first occurred over Antarctica. In 1987 nations negotiated the Montreal Protocol in order to avoid enlarging the ozone hole. The U.N. Secretary-General called the treaty "perhaps the single most successful international agreement to date."

The protocol went into effect in 1989, only four years after the problem was first discovered. If the nations could agree on an environmental danger and effectively ban the harmful substances that caused it, perhaps they could respond to other scientific warnings. Dangers to the environment did not appear to be a partisan issue in the U.S., at least in the past. It was President Nixon who recommended the Environmental Protection Agency in 1970, and President Reagan who asked the Senate to ratify the Montreal agreement in 1987.

However, in the case of chlorofluorocarbons, a cause of the ozone hole, replacements were available, and in the case of the pollution of the late 1960s, the problem was obvious to many ordinary citizens, in the form, for example, of toxins in rivers, smog in the air. One of the factors that makes the greenhouse gas crisis so hard is that the cause is invisible, the effect is delayed, the cure requires international cooperation and, apart from so-far-unknown technology, a change in our way of life. Also, fossil fuels are now the largest single industry in the world, and these firms have a strong economic interest in not recognizing the problem or, to the extent it is seen, not doing anything adequate about it.

An observer might be excused for saying the situation is impossible. But that is what they said about ending the Cold War in the mid 1980s. It is my own judgment that dealing with climate change will be at least as daunting, but might turn out to be no less doable, at least to the extent of delaying and lessening its worst effects. I don't know what it will take, but it will surely take more than politics as usual. The future will be very different, in any case out of our comfort zone. The question is, will we design the future or suffer it?

OVERSHOOT

If the two major U.S. parties could unite to clean up rivers and ban ozone-destroying chemicals, could our leaders not respond effectively to today's environmental challenges?

The success of the Montreal Protocol to do the latter was deceptive, because in that case, economical substitutes could be found for the chemicals dangerous to the ozone layer, chemicals manufactured by a small number of firms. In contrast, how do we control population, and how do we diminish greenhouse gases emitted, among other sources, by power plants burning fossil fuel and by millions of vehicle tailpipes and furnaces?

In *Overshoot: the Ecological Basis of Revolutionary Change*, William F. Catton writes about such concepts as carrying capacity, the cornucopian myth, and what he calls "cargoism," the delusion that technology will always save us. Save us from what? From growth beyond an area's carrying capacity, leading to die-off.

Cargoism refers to the "cargo cults" of some Pacific islands which first saw shiploads of modern goods during the Second World War and assumed that more ships could be caused to land, bringing wealth. Catton is concerned with the assumption that technology will always deliver what we need, as the ships brought abundant and marvelous goods. He starts by writing about wishful dreaming.

Published as long ago as 1980, his book was a severe wake-up call, like a smoke alarm going off in the night. What he was saying is that if technology doesn't save us (or if it creates even worse problems), our religion of eternal economic growth will lead to a crash and, as it says right on the front cover of his book, to the "die-off" of part of the population.

It is natural for a population that has overshot its resource base to expand in numbers, after which the die-off suddenly reduces the numbers for a while even below what is sustainable. If you combine Catton's argument with ecological footprint analysis, billions could die, in this century, before their normal life expectancies.

I viewed the effort to help end the Cold War, a change that depended on many things coming together, only as a prudent step toward surviving long enough to deal with the challenges that Catton and other observers explain.

"Cornucopians" assume technology will always come to the rescue, like the cavalry riding in, and some have even argued that a higher level of population is a cause for celebration because it means more geniuses are likely. They point out that England needed radar to stop German air attacks, and the U.S. needed a nuclear bomb to make it unnecessary to invade Japan, and presto, we developed them.

But of course technology did not save Hitler's "Thousand Year Reich," though the Nazis tried to synthesize fuel and to attack England by new and terrible means. Technology has given us the iPhone and marvels of even greater scope than "Siri," but there are many problems that it has not been able, so far, to solve. Technology has not yet prevented the growth of population. It has not yet provided a new safe energy source with the density and portability of gasoline and kerosene. It has not yet provided a flow of affordable fresh water. In the case of many people, it has not been able to save them from hunger and disease.

Many of us felt at least as early as the 1990s that "progress" was not assured. Yes, we could substitute our way around some shortages, and invent new technologies that made more efficient use of what we had. Yes, the organization of science and technology seemed to assure we'd soon be able to do certain things that had seemed like magic, if they had even been imagined.

But back to Catton: his book is about stealing from the future or engaging in unsustainable development, again as if some unknown development would surely rescue our progeny from the otherwise dismal consequences. It's unthinkable that, like a playboy spending his inheritance on trivia, we'd produce a future without the resources to support it.

We had a preview of Catton's warning as early as 1972, in the form of *The Limits to Growth*.[5] This book was quickly misrepresented and dismissed, as it clearly challenged our widely shared civic religion of endless economic growth. In another age, the authors might have been burned at the stake. As it was, a possible scenario was misrepresented as a prediction. We were assured that more would always be available if the price was high enough, and in any case, that one resource could almost always be replaced, if necessary, by another. Mainstream economics savaged the book, which challenged some of the basic assumptions of that discipline.

Most dangerous, perhaps. the economic elite has depended on the myth of eternal growth to take the pressure off calls for less inequality: if things were getting a little better regularly for everyone, couldn't the elite "contain" complaints that some had much more than others?

It's possible that our species is both overshooting the numbers that can be comfortably supported on the planet, and also losing tolerance for gross inequality. As changes in the climate become more obvious, we may have to consider the question of how to live with less purchasing power. Our ultimate goal is not having stuff, but feeling happy. Are there ways to increase our happiness?

REDEFINING WEALTH

In the editor's letter[6] in the inaugural issue of the *Elmwood Quarterly*, I used the metaphor of the cornucopia to discuss an emerging challenge. What is so startling, more than twenty years later, is that the challenges are now more familiar, but far from being met. Perhaps part of resilience is being willing to adopt a different goal, a new dream, when the old one is no longer appropriate. Here is part of that letter:

> Let lovers of Gaia recall, as the ancient Greeks did, how the goddess of this name gave birth to Zeus. Hid from his murderous father, the baby was nursed with milk from a goat. One of the goat's horns, broken off, became the first cornucopia, yielding whatever nourishment its possessor desired, including ambrosia (the food of the gods).

American art has generally depicted the cornucopia as spilling forth abundant fruits and vegetables and amber waves of grain—a satisfying glyph for those whom historian David Potter called the "people of plenty." In a similar spirit, political candidates have long promised us an ever-rising "standard of living." In 1952, for example, Eisenhower pledged not only an end to the Korean war, but also "progress and prosperity."

In the past twenty years, our affluent identity has been threatened by oil shocks, income stagnation, and the relative economic rise of Japan and then of China. Some observers would say that our national response so far has been (a) to go on boasting that we're the greatest, (b) to celebrate small government while borrowing massively and hoisting a bigger military stick, and (c) to shift 60% or more of the new wealth to 1% of the population—presumably as an encouraging symbol of anyone's chance to get rich.

In a few years the U.S. has gone from fearing the Soviet military to feeling perturbed that certain other countries are developing an economy bigger than our own. It's no longer enough to keep growing relative to past performance; now Americans worry about other people developing faster than we are.

Asked to name a system suffused with propaganda and committed to taking over the world, most Americans would think of pre-Gorbachev communism. But in another sense this description applies to advanced industrial society. The propaganda tells us to consume what the system profits by producing, and to pay for it by working at the kinds of jobs the system makes available, as if to say "You can get anything you want at marketplace restaurant."

Nevertheless, several developments now encourage us to question the value of consumerism. People are again wondering: despite the success of our economic cornucopia, is it failing to yield some of the most essential goods, services, and social arrangements? What about a sense of community—at which boutique is that being sold? What about "quality time"? At which discount warehouse can you get a good deal on friendships? What about "safe streets"?

Defining wealth as the ability to buy things, we have largely lost the sense of "weal," which means well-being (as in the word "commonweal"). To most people, wealth now refers less to shared well-being than to "gross national product" or "personal net worth."

Questions are being raised not only about whether we're getting what we need, but also whether we can go on producing in the ways we do. Are there environmental limits to our present type of economic growth? If a certain pattern of economic activity has the "side effect" of fouling earth, air, and water, or altering global climate in ominous ways, how do we assess the wealth thus created? With regard to greenhouse gases, are we involved in a replay of the tobacco fiasco, where companies argued for decades that "no conclusive evidence" proved a link between smoking and disease?

How much risk are we willing to take to keep using fossil fuels in a profligate way? When President Carter wore a sweater and urged energy efficiency, he was accused by Reagan of wanting us to shiver in the cold and the dark. Is it wealth to be able to waste energy? Is it wealth to get certain things now only at the cost of harming future generations?

Sometimes I ask people what would happen if the U.S., in some unhappy circumstance, had to cut consumption. In this thought experiment, I find that most people are somewhat disturbed by imagining a 10% cut, disoriented by 25%, and utterly horrified by 50%. Wouldn't society collapse? In generational terms, however, it was not so long ago that we were actually living at each of these lower levels of consumption. And for most of the world, having half as much per capita as Americans do now, would feel like paradise.

What are the values that animate our lives, apart from being rich? What do we stand for besides standing at the cornucopia's outlet? There are many possible answers. Which ones would you give? (*Elmwood Quarterly*, Spring Equinox, 1992)

THE BEST PREP

If my forties had a lesson for me, it was simple: life could become much richer if I deliberately and voluntarily ventured outside my comfort zone. It has not escaped my notice that this practice also serves as the best preparation for being thrown outside our comfort zones, if that should occur in the future. Going outside the zone and thriving can become a gracious habit.

Having a well-defined comfort zone might be comfortable but it isn't necessarily resilient. A familiar zone lowers anxiety, but it doesn't teach adaptability. If our goal is to discover more of the plenitude of life, it's surely useful to learn to go outside our comfort zones. In this book, most of my examples were positive, but in case of a setback, it is also positive to learn how to recover and try something else.

If I were facing a challenge, such as travel in unknown lands, I'd want a companion who was resilient, in preference to someone who knew how to do one thing well but was afraid to try anything else. To the extent that the future promises to be turbulent and surprising, the best thing we can do now is to make a practice of going voluntarily outside our present comfort zones.

At the end of the period of this memoir, in 1992, several challenges were already forming that seemed daunting but were arguably no more "impossible" than moderating the manifestly dangerous Cold War that lapsed in the late 1980s. Meanwhile, we can enrich our lives by getting into the habit of taking on new changes voluntarily.

Notes

INTRODUCTION:

1. Yo-yo Ma: Like millions of others, I admire the cellist Yo-yo Ma. Apart from his classical music, he supports the Silk Road Ensemble and made a playful and lovely album with Bobby McFerrin (who once performed at a party for a pair of books that I had edited with entrepreneur Don Carlson). On the UC Berkeley campus I had the pleasure of attending "Falling Down Stairs," a Mark Morris dance performance. On the left side of the proscenium arch, in the shadows, without a music stand, was a cellist. Not being able to see the musician's face, I consulted the program. It was Yo-yo Ma, who on that evening knew the focus should be elsewhere. Ma also worked with the music of Philip Glass, who figures in Chapter 4 of this book.

2. Trying something new: In the early 1970s I became co-director of the William James Center on Adult Development in Berkeley, which, for example, was instrumental in creating the report, *Faculty Development in a Time of Retrenchment*. Probably the most popular book on "mid-life crisis" at the time was Gail Sheehy's deeply-informed *Passages*, which came out in 1978, just before the period described in this book. In its December 2014 issue The *Atlantic* magazine published "The Real Roots of Midlife Crisis," by Jonathan Rauch.

3. William James Center for Adult Development: A program of the Wright Institute, a center for research and teaching in clinical-social psychology in Berkeley, California, which also ran a graduate school (see the story in the Introduction about starting the school).

4. Bill Kauth: Probably the best known of his social inventions is the Mankind Project (MKP), which offers an intensive training in mature masculinity and has over 60,000 graduates around the world.

5. Grief: One of the most lucid authorities on grief is Francis Weller, author of *The Wild Edge of Sorrow: Rituals of Renewal and the Sacred Work of Grief* and also of the Foreword to my book, *Gift of Darkness: Growing Up in Occupied Amsterdam*.

6. Hedonic adaptation: See, for example, Sonia Lyubomirsky, *Hedonic Adaptation to Positive and Negative Experience* (Oxford, 2010).

7. Recommended by our staff: This happy accident was perhaps made possible by a staff whose taste was similar to my own.

8. Openness to experience: An extensive literature exists. Some of the classic studies are by R.R. McCrae. The lead author of a research paper on twins is K.L. Jang.

9. A new book: *Citizen Summitry: Keeping The Peace When It Matters Too Much To Be Left To Politicians* was edited by Don Carlson and Craig K. Comstock and contained at least thirty-five pages of contributions from Soviet authors who were invited not to repeat the usual peace line but to envision links, after the Cold War, between our two countries.

10. Co-author: This was yet another of the remarkable men with whom I had the honor of working, Nevitt Sanford, himself co-author of the classic, *The Authoritarian Personality*.

The book we did together was *Sanctions for Evil: Sources of Social Destructiveness* (published by Jossey-Bass in 1971, and in the next year in paperback by Beacon Press) with research support from Norman Cohn, author of *The Pursuit of the Millennium*.

11. Adventure story: Some adventure stories describe climbing mountains or, in my brother's case, piloting hot air balloons (*A Life in the Air*); others are about such things as international politics or self-understanding.

12. Habit of learning: This is related to practices described by Twyla Tharp in *The Creative Habit: Learn It and Use It For Life* (2003).

13. Flow: For the concept of "flow" see Chapter 2 "The Transition."

14. David Riesman: Author of *The Lonely Crowd*, he gave a Harvard course called "American Character and Social Structure," and invited me to teach one of the sections. With the rest of the staff, I attended a weekly dinner at Riesman's home, at which we exchanged stories about teaching, discussed the reading for the coming week, and conversed with such guests as Ken Boulding, Erik Erikson, and Ken Keniston.

CHAPTER 1 (Wake-Up Calls)

1. Alzheimer's Syndrome: One source of expert information on this syndrome is the Mayo clinic in Rochester, Minnesota, near where my Dad grew up.

2. Life-world: What the Germans call *lebenswelt*, it is the environment as experienced by a particular animal, whether for example a bat or a dolphin.

3. Dolphins: Though trained as a medical doctor not as a student of animal behavior, John C. Lilly was much quoted in the period of this memoir for his work on what he later called "humans of the sea": for example, *The Mind of the Dolphin* (Doubleday, 1967).

4. Fishing captain: I owe this story to the San Francisco Bay Area businessman and philanthropist Don Carlson (see Chapter 6).

5. Yosal Rogat: His papers included *The Eichmann Trial and the Rule of Law* (Center for the Study of Democratic Institutions, 1961); "Mr. Justice Holmes: A Dissenting Opinion," part one, *Stanford Law Review* 15:1, pp. 3-44 (December 1962); part two. *Stanford Law Review* 15:2, pp. 254-308 (March 1963); "Mr. Justice Pangloss," *New York Review of Books* (October 11, 1964), "The Judge as Spectator," *University of Chicago Law Review* 31:2, pp. 213-256 (1964); "Legal Realism," *Enyclopedia of Philosophy*, pp.420-421 (Macmillan and Free Press, 1967); "I'm All Right, Dick," *New York Review of Books,* (September 21, 1972); and posthumously, with James M. O'Fallon, "Mr. Justice Holes: A Dissenting Opinion—The Speech Cases," *Stanford Law Review* 36:1349 (1984). Among scholars, citations suggest the extent to which a writer's arguments live. One recent example is "Beyond tragedy: Arendt, Rogat, and the Judges in Jerusalem," by Sussanah Young-ah Gottlieb, which appeared in *College Literature,* 38:1, pp. 45-56 (winter 2011).

6. Modernisms: At the time, the number of studies of modernism as a whole was limited. One early title was *Faces of Modernity: Modernism, Avante Garde, Decadence, Kitsch, Postmodernism,* by the Roumanian scholar Matei Calinescu (Indiana, 1977). Much later, it was possible to read a number of studies such as *Modernism: A Literary Guide* by Peter Nicolls (Palgrave/Macmillan, 1995), *Modernism: The Lure of Heresy* by Peter Gay (Norton, 2007), *The Cambridge Introduction to Modernism* by Pericles Lewis (Cambridge, 2007), and *Modernism: A Very Short Introduction* by Christopher Butler (Oxford, 2010). None of these books ventures much beyond literature or literature and other arts.

7. *Citizen Kane*: The script was written for Orson Wells by Herman Mankiewicz. His son Frank was Yosal's friend at UCLA and later, in his professional life, a Peace Corps executive, a journalist, and an aide to Robert Kennedy.

CHAPTER 2 (The Transition)

1. *Drawing on the Right Side of the Brain:* Published in 1979 by Jeremy Tarcher (who later issued a pair of books that were co-edited by Don Carlson and me).

2. Alter Klang: While "klang" literally refers to "sound," according to a curator's note in the Bauhaus exhibit at the Barbican, London, 2012, Kandinsky said that his colleague Paul Klee used the word as a reference to "soul." Thus, the title of Klee's painting might be rendered as "ancient soul."

3. Report on the 25th anniversary: Most of this unit was originally published in *Harvard College Class of 1961: 25th Anniversary Report* (Cambridge, 1986).

4. When I asked the dean: See the biography called *John U. Monro: Uncommon Educator* by Toni-Lee Capossela (Louisiana State University Press, 2012).

5. Favorite Harvard authors: Apart from Stanley Cavell's and F.O. Matthiesson's books, see Robert Sullivan, *The Thoreau You Don't Know* (Collins, 2009), which shows Thoreau less as a hermit than as a man trying to simplify his life so he could find out what was important, a challenge best not left until old age.

6. ***Worse Than Futile:*** This was a stand-alone report written by me about the "loyalty affidavit" and oath required by Congress in National Defense Education Act. Published by the Harvard *Crimson* it was widely distributed within U.S. higher education.

7. **Sojourn in that cabin:** In the *New Yorker* (October 19, 2015), Kathryn Schulz contributed a well-crafted piece called "Pond Scum," in which she expressed her skepticism about Thoreau as a hero and even likened his reliance upon the self to that of Ayn Rand. Much as I enjoyed her valuable comments on Thoreau's character, the article does little to explain the contributions made by the author of *Walden* and other works. For example, the article claims that "he wanted to try what we would today call subsistence living, a condition attractive chiefly to those not obliged to endure it." In my view, Thoreau went to an extreme to offer a contrast to the normality of a proto-consumerist culture.

8. **Went to the woods:** See page 394 in the Library of America's collection of Thoreau's main works.

9. **Mihaly Cziksentmihalyi:** The books of his that most influenced me were *Beyond Boredom and Anxiety* (Jossey-Bass, 1975) and later *Flow: The Psychology of Optimal Experience* (Harper and Row, 1990).

10. **Vicki Noble:** Harper San Francisco published the first edition of *Motherpeace: A Way to the Goddess Through Myth, Art, and Tarot in* 1982.

11. **The "fool" card:** A recent example of a fool in the halls of power is the 2006 talk by Stephen Colbert to the White House Correspondents dinner, attended by President Bush the younger. In his right-wing persona, Colbert pretended

to identify with Bush as a person who proudly made decisions "from the gut," not from mere facts found in books. "Reality," Colbert observed, "has a well-known liberal bias." See the easily available video of his talk to the White House Correspondents Association dinner in 2006, at which he addressed the President a few chairs away and appeared to shock many listeners by performing as a Shakespearean fool.

12. Enneagram: One useful book is by Helen Palmer, whom, as a stranger, I once went to meet in a small group on a different matter. As soon as I'd walked through the door, she pointed at me, across a large room, and exclaimed, "Five." To the extent this was true, I hadn't known it was so obvious. Her basic book is *The Enneagram: Understanding Yourself and the Others in Your Life* (Center for the Investigation and Training of Intuition, 1988; HarperCollins, 1991)

13. Beginner's mind: Shunryo Suzuki, *Zen Mind, Beginner's Mind* (Weatherhill, 1973). The Japanese is *shoshin*.

CHAPTER 3 (A Tantric Initiation)

1. Margo Anand: As she was then known, without the final "t" on her first name, Margo wasn't alone in bringing some kind of tantric understanding to the West. Charles and Caroline Muir's *Tantra: The Art of Conscious Loving* had appeared in 1969, Jolan Chang's *The Tao of Love and Sex*, in 1977; Nik Douglas and Penny Slinger's *Sexual Secrets*, in 1979. Tarcher published Margo's widely read American book in 1989, but her related French book had come out back in 1981. Mantak Chia and Michael Winn's *Taoist Secrets of Love* appeared in 1984, as did Keith Dowman's *Sky Dancer: The Secret Life and Songs of Lady Yeshe Tsogyel;* and David and Ellen Ramsdale's *Sexual Energy Ecstasy* in

1985. Another scholarly book useful for understanding what Margo calls "sky-dancing tantra" is Miranda Shaw's *Passionate Enlightenment: Women in Tantric Buddhism*, published in 1994.

I would encourage readers to check out Margo's books, which convey her meaning directly and which include ideas expressed after we worked together.

2. Bhagwan Shree Rajneesh: Author of many books, this guru, later called Osho, wrote *Tantra: The Supreme Understanding*, originally published as *Only One Sky* in 1975 and available in many editions (most recently Watkins, 2009).

CHAPTER 4 (A Glorious Surprise)

1. Da Free John: The autobiography that describes his spiritual awakening is *The Knee of Listening* (Dawn Horse Press, 1972). I read the first edition, which I regard as much superior to later revisions and expansions by the author.

2. Brother-in-law: His name was Richard Kohn, the director of a documentary film, *Lord of the Dance/Destroyer of Illusion*, shown in the U.S. on the National Geographic channel and widely in Europe; and author of *Lord of the Dance: The Mani Rimdu Festival in Tibet and Nepal* (State University of New York Press, published posthumously in 2001).

3. *Koyaanisqatsi*: This film was directed by Godfrey Reggio and released in 1982 with the subtitle of *Life Out of Balance*. It was the first in a trilogy that continued with *Powaqqatsi* (1988) and *Naqoyqatsi* (2002).

4. Happiness: This concept and closely related concepts have popped up repeatedly, as in the philosophy of Marcus Aurelius, in Thomas Jefferson's famous Declaration ("life, liberty, and the pursuit of happiness"), and current "positive psychology" exemplified by Dacher Keltner and Martin Seligman.

5. Ineffable: A vast literature has been generated, mainly by philosophers and theologians, on the subject of things said to be impossible to describe in language. Some of it is valuable, but not all of these writers have suffered a relevant experience. I have started with an experience, rather than a theory of language.

6. Stan and Christina Grof: Two books that illuminate the "transformational crisis" are by the team of Christina Grof and Stan Grof, the first with the husband as primary author, the second with the wife as primary: *Spiritual Emergency: When Personal Transformation Becomes a Crisis* (1989) and *The Stormy Search for the Self: A Guide to Personal Growth Through Transformational Crisis* (1990).

7. Out-of-body experience: There is now a considerable literature on what are interpreted as out-of-body experiences, pioneered by Raymond A. Moody, author of books alone and with Elizabeth Kubler-Ross, Paul Perry, and Neale Donald Walsh. Moody's main book came in 1975.

CHAPTER 5 (Family Dynamics)

1. Quadrinity Process: In chronological order, two descriptions of the Process by teachers are *Journey into Love* by Kani Comstock and Marissa Thames (Willow Press, 2000), and *The Hoffman Process* by Tim Laurence (Bantam, 2004). Disclosure: the first book is by my sister; the second, by a friend.

2. Bob Hoffman: The book that Bob wanted to revise appeared as *No One is to Blame: Freedom from Compulsive Self-defeating Behavior* (Science and Behavior Books, third edition, 1988).

3. Daughters of the American Revolution: Franklin D. Roosevelt is supposed to have said: "remember always that all of us, and you and I especially, are descended from immigrants and revolutionists."

CHAPTER 6 (Ark)

1. *Guns of August*: See Dobbs, Michael *One Minute to Midnight* (2008), pp. 226–227: "The President was so impressed by the [Tuchman] book that he often quoted from it, and insisted [that] his aides read it. He wanted 'every officer in the Army' to read it as well. The secretary of the Army sent copies to every U.S. military base in the world."

2. *The Day After*: This made-for-TV movie was seen by more than 100 million people on its first broadcast on ABC in 1983. A friend tells me he watched in a group, having been warned the movie might induce depression in a solitary viewer.

3. One of our books: The excerpt is taken from *Citizen Summitry: Keeping the Peace When It Matters Too Much to be Left to Politicians,* edited by Don Carlson and Craig Comstock (Tarcher, 1986), pages 10-13.

4. Air Force museum: National Museum of the Air Force at Wright Patterson Field near Dayton, Ohio.

5. "Rubble bounce": This phrase is attributed to Winston Churchill, and was said to have been picked up, and expanded, by General Curtis LeMay, commander of the U.S. Strategic Air Command.

6. The Committee for a Sane Nuclear Policy: See *Ban the Bomb: A History of SANE*, by Milton S. Katz (Praeger, 1987).

CHAPTER 7 (Meeting the Other Side):

1. Secret notes on the conference: Both the U.S. and the Soviet notes on the negotiations, previously secret, edited by Dr. Svetlana Savranskaya and Thomas Blanton, are available at the National Security Archive on the internet at: http://www.gwu.edu/~nsarchiv/NSAEBB/NSAEBB203/index.htm

2. A key adviser to Khrushchev: This was Fyodor Burlatsky, cited repeatedly in Archie Brown's book, *The Gorbachev Factor* (Oxford University Press, 1997), my main guide in Chapter 7.

3. *Fog of War*: With a subtitle of "Eleven Lessons from the Life of Robert S. McNamara," this is a documentary film made by Errol Morris, featuring the former Secretary of Defense, and released in 2003. The title is an allusion to the Prussian military analyst Carl von Clausewitz.

4. Wall of Shame and Barbed Wire: The phrase "Schandmauer und Stacheldraht" is ascribed to Willy Brandt, whom I once had the honor, as a college kid, of hosting at a dinner around 1960. Brandt became mayor of West Berlin, then chancellor of the Federal Republic of Germany, and in 1971 winner of the Nobel Prize for Peace.

5. Sharon Tennison: In 1983, in San Francisco, Tennison founded the Center for US-USSR Initiatives, which after the dissolution of the Soviet state, became the Center for Citizen Initiatives. Her history of this enterprise is called *The Power of Impossible Ideas: Ordinary Citizens' Extraordinary Efforts to Avert International Crisis* (Oldenwald Press, 2012).

6. American University: Called "A Strategy of Peace" and delivered on June 10, 1963, this speech appears in *Securing Our Planet*, edited by Don Carlson and Craig Comstock (Tarcher, 1984), pp. 33-39, and can now be seen on YouTube.

CHAPTER 8 (Openess to Experience)

1. *Learning After College:* Was published by Montaigne, Inc., in 1980.

2. Multiple choice test: In his 2016 movie about "invading" countries to bring back ideas for social reforms in the U.S., Michael Moore talks with Finnish teachers about the folly of using multiple-choice exams to discover which schools are good. The Finns tell him, all our schools are good. It's illegal there to have anything but public schools, so everyone has an interest in making them excellent. The documentary also visits Italy (guaranteeing paid vacations), France (serving healthy and appealing school lunches), Germany (coming to terms with evils in the past, putting workers on company boards), Portugal (ending a war on drugs), Tunisia (expelling a tyrant), Norway (building humane prisons), Slovenia (offering free higher education), and Iceland (prosecuting bankers, bringing women to power).

3. Beginner's mind: Working with Trudy Dixon in the first edition, and with David Chadwick in a revised edition, Susuki Roshi wrote *Zen Mind, Beginner's Mind: Informal Talks on Zen Meditation and Practice*, published in 1993 and in 2011, respectively.

4. Hot air ballooning: Bruce Comstock's account of these adventures is *A Life in the Air*, published in 2013.

5. Kani Comstock's books: *Journey into Love* was published in English in 2000 (and is also available in Portugese and Spanish). *Honoring Missed Motherhood: Loss, Choice, and Creativity*, in 2013 (in collaboration with Barbara Comstock).

6. Try it now: Don't be turned away just because the project seems "impossible." (See Chapter 6 about Ark.) One of the pioneer citizen diplomats whom we supported was Sharon Tennison, who called her book *The Power of Impossible Ideas*. One of my clients, writing on citizen action, came up with a title inspired by a Billie Holiday line, *The Impossible Will Take a Little While*. The Czech who rose from dissident to President of his country called one of his books *The Art of the Impossible: Politics as Morality in Practice*. Some projects don't work, but humans have a bad record at predicting what will succeed.

APPENDIX (Scenarios)

1. Elmwood Institute: Founded by Fritjof Capra in 1984, this institute was located in Berkeley, California, and was followed in spirit by the Center for Ecoliteracy, directed by Zenobia Barlow.

2. Ernest (Chick) Callenbach: Author of the best-selling *Ecotopia* (1975), which he self-published after it was rejected by many publishers, and author of such other forward-leaning books as *Ecotopia Emerging* (1981), *A Citizen Legislature* (1985), *Living Cheaply With Style* (1993), *Ecology: A Pocket Guide* (1998), *Bring Back the Buffalo* (2000).

3. *Elmwood Quarterly*: A list of writers in that first year included such names as Ernest Callenbach, Fritjof Capra, Hugh R. Downs, Duane Elgin, Jordan Fisher-Smith, Chellis Glendinning, Randy Hayes, Hazel Henderson, Satish Kumar,

Dolores LaChapelle, Arne Naess, Helena Norberg-Hodge, David W. Orr, Michael Pollan, Bill Reid, John Seed, George Sessions, Gary Snyder, Mark Sommer, Charlene Spetnak, and David Steindl-Rast. I don't know how many of these writers are widely known; they all deserve to be.

4. Denial practiced almost unconsciously by many readers: Some of the classics on the difficulty humans (and especially far-right wingers) have of listening to unwelcome warnings from science include Chris Mooney, *The Republican War on Science* (2007) and *The Republican Brain: The Science of Why They Deny Science—and Reality* (2012), and Eric N. Conway and Naomi Oreskes, *Merchants of Doubt* (2011) and the same pair of authors in reverse order, *The Collapse of Western Civilization* (2014), an expansion of an article in *Daedalus* (January 2013).

5. The Limits to Growth: Like Rachel Carson's *Silent Spring,* this critique of the civic religion of "progress" was fiercely attacked upon publication. Sponsored by the Club of Rome, *Limits* was written by Donella H. Meadows, Dennis L. Meadows, Jorgen Randers, and William W. Behrens III. Theologians in the church of perpetual economic growth, led by conventional economists, found the premise of *Limits* unthinkable or stupid: among other rhetorical tricks, or mistakes, some of them treated a possible "scenario" as if it were a "prediction."

Published as long ago as 1972, and discredited for a while by a barrage of unfair criticism, the book has been re-evaluated by Matthew R. Simmons, "Revisiting the Limits to Growth: Could the Club of Rome Have Been Right, After All?" *Energy Bulletin* (2000); by Charles A.S. Hall and John W. Day, "Revisiting the Limits to Growth After Peak Oil,"

American Scientist, volume 97, number 3 (2009); and by Ugo Bardi, *The Limits to Growth Revisited* (Springer, 2011).

6. Editor's letter: Originally published in *Elmwood Quarterly* in 1992, this piece was picked up by the website called Resilience.org twenty years later and republished on April 25, 2012.

INDEX

accident xv, 16, 18, 21, 23, 106, 172
adventure xiii, xv, 97, 148, 173
Alferenko, Gennady 139
Allen, Woody 28
Alzheimer's 3, 4, 8, 16, 68, 173
American University 140, 182
Anand, Margo[t] 49, 50-57, 60, 86, 177, 178, 191
Ann Arbor (Michigan) 4, 97
Arendt, Hannah 11, 174
Ark iii, ix, 29, 52, 101, 103, 105-107, 109, 111, 113-115, 117-119, 123, 124, 128, 137, 138, 140, 180, 183, 193
art 8, 9, 23-25, 41, 44, 49, 51, 96, 146, 149, 167, 176, 177, 183
Ashland (Oregon) vi, 191
authoritarian xvii, 172
avalanche 20
awkward xi, xii, xiv, 75, 147
Bauhaus 25, 175
Bay Area (San Francisco) 1, 5, 9, 41, 42, 53, 60-62, 68, 95, 151, 174, 193
Berlin (Germany) 25, 53, 135, 136, 181
Berlin Wall 107, 135, 136, 139, 181
Bill of Rights 127, 140
black swan event 134
book creation coach xii, xiii, xvi, 13, 26, 38, 41, 42, 71, 75, 83, 95, 105, 151, 191, 193
Buddhist 40, 45, 62, 67, 87, 147
Bundy, McGeorge 130
Burlatsky, Fyodor 181
Business Executives for National Security (BENS) 106
Cabo San Lucas (Mexico) 8
Carlson, Don iii, vi, xiv, 53, 105, 107, 114, 128, 171, 172, 174, 175, 180, 182, 191

challenge xiv, xviii, xx, 24, 35, 37, 38, 44, 56, 89, 98, 102, 125, 134, 136, 149, 151, 153, 154, 157, 158, 160, 161, 163-166, 169, 170, 175
Chernobyl xiii, 128, 134
citizen diplomacy xi, 112-115, 119, 127, 129, 137, 140, 141
Citizen Summitry iii, vi, xiii, 29, 52, 101, 105, 122, 125, 172, 180
citizen summitry 108, 111
clients vii, xii, 26, 40-43, 73, 75, 86, 107, 151, 183, 193
Close, Chuck vi, 65
Colbert, Stephen 87, 176, 177
Cold War xi, xiii-xv, xx, 5, 52, 95, 101, 106, 107, 111, 112, 114-117, 126-128, 135, 137, 141, 142, 151, 163, 164, 170, 172
Cold Warrior xiv
collapse xi, xviii, 19, 91, 147, 156-158, 169, 184
comfort zone vii, xi-xv, xviii, xix, xxiii, 42, 45, 57, 70, 101, 148, 149, 163, 169, 170
Comfort, Alex 54, 55
Committee for a Sane Nuclear Policy (SANE) 112, 181
Committee for Nuclear Disarmament (CND) 112
Comstock, Barbara 1, 148, 183, 191
Comstock, Bruce 4, 5, 35, 90, 91, 182, 191
Comstock, Kani vi, 1, 4, 39, 69, 78, 85, 88, 148, 179, 183, 191
Comstock, Marge (Mom) 1, 3, 4, 6, 68, 90, 92, 93, 95-98, 191
Comstock, Roy (Dad) xvii, 1-8, 50, 62, 76, 89-91, 95, 96, 173, 191
Concord (Massachusetts) 33
consumer culture 57

Csikszentmihalyi, Mihaly 34, 176
Cuban Missile Crisis 102, 103, 109, 128, 129, 131-133, 135, 136, 142, 159
death exposures 19
dementia 3, 6, 7, 23
Dissanayake, Ellen 36
Dobbs, Michael 130, 180
doctorate 9, 10, 148, 191
ecstasy 49-51, 57, 65, 71, 75, 177
Eichmann trial 15, 174
Elgin, Duane 36, 184
empathy 85, 126, 140
energy 23, 56, 66, 68, 72, 73, 126, 149, 155, 156, 158, 165, 168, 177, 184
Esalen Institute 112, 113, 140
family of origin xi, 148
flow xviii, 34, 35, 64, 66, 67, 69, 70, 95, 165, 173, 176
Fonda, Jane 119
fool 38, 123, 147, 176, 177
Frank Knox Fellowship 193
Free John, Da 61, 178
glasnost 123, 127, 128, 131
Glass, Philip vi, 64, 65, 72, 171, 191
Gorbachev, Mikhail vi, xiii, 108, 114, 121, 123, 124, 127, 128, 130, 136, 139, 141, 167, 181
Gregory, Andre 13, 16
Grof, Christina and Stan 73, 179, 191
Grotowski, Jerzy 14
Haas, Richard 116, 117
happiness xi, 71, 153, 166, 178, 179
Harvard iii, xvi, 28, 29, 94, 97, 102, 173, 175, 176, 191, 193
Hayden, Tom 119
hedonic adaptation xi, 172
Hoffman Quadrinity Process 83-89, 91, 92, 179
Hoffman, Bob 83, 86, 87, 180, 191
Hofmann, Albert 59, 60

Holmes, Oliver Wendell 10, 12, 14, 174
hot air ballooning 6, 34, 35, 91, 95, 148, 173, 183
impossible xiv, xx, 44, 71, 86, 103, 124, 128, 137, 139, 163, 170, 179, 181, 182
ineffable 71, 74, 179
interior design 88, 96, 97
Ischgl (Austria) 18, 19, 21
James, William 59
Journey into Love 85, 148, 179, 183
Kealakekua Bay (Hawaii) 7
Kennedy, John F. (JFK) iii, 30, 103, 104, 130, 131, 132, 133, 136, 140
Khrushchev, Nikita 128, 130, 131, 133, 181
King, Jr., Martin Luther 31
Kissinger, Henry 102, 104
Klee, Paul 25, 175
Kohn, Richard 178, 191
Koyaanisqatsi 62, 63, 66, 70, 74, 75, 178
Laing, R.D. 73
learning xii, xvi, xvii, 12, 21, 28, 61, 91, 145-147, 149, 173
Learning After College 41, 145, 182
Lenin xiv, 128
life-worlds 7, 8
Louisiana Purchase 40
loyalty iii, 30, 93, 176
luck xi, xv, xix, 132, 134, 146
Luther, Martin 50
MacLaine, Shirley 26, 115, 191
Malle, Louis 13, 16
McCarthy, Senator Joseph 30, 78
McNamara, Robert 129, 130-134, 181
memoir xii, xiii, xv, 68, 139, 170, 174
Mills, C. Wright 93

INDEX

Milwaukee (Wisconsin) 25, 78, 81, 93
Minnesota 2, 89, 173
modernisms 9, 10, 13, 174
Montaigne 182
Moscow (USSR) xiii, xiv, 43, 111, 116-118, 121, 123, 125-130, 132, 134, 137, 138, 140, 141
Motherpeace vi, 23, 38, 39, 176
My Dinner with Andre 13, 14, 16
national security elite 104, 114, 141
New York City xvi, 79, 91, 93, 94
New York Review of Books 11, 62, 174
Nixon, President Richard 102, 162
Noble, Vicki vi, 23, 38, 39, 176, 191
nuclear weapons (such as "Fat Man") 102, 104, 115, 122, 123, 130-134, 141, 142, 159, 162
openness to experience ix, xiii, xvii, xviii, 145, 172
out-of-body experience (OBE) 79, 80, 179
Physicians for Social Responsibility 112, 137
Picasso, Pablo 10
play 8, 11, 13, 25, 35-37, 57, 76, 91, 119, 126, 135
Point Reyes (north of San Francisco) 51
Popper, Karl 77
Provence (France) 54
psychic 62
psychologist xvii, 9, 29, 34, 88, 191
Pugwash 112
Rajneesh, Bhagwan Shree 50, 53, 76, 178
Ram Dass 61
Reagan, Ronald vi, xiii, 104, 115, 116, 121, 123, 129, 130, 136, 162, 168
real estate 4, 88, 95, 97, 105
Reggio, Godfrey 72, 178

Reykjavik (Iceland) xiii, 115, 116, 118, 121, 122, 130
Riefenstahl, Leni 60
Riesman, David xx, 173, 191
Rogat, Yosal 9-16, 174, 191
Roosevelt, Franklin D. (FDR) 94, 180
Russell, Lord Bertrand 113
San Francisco (California) xiv, 1, 9, 11, 41, 42, 51-53, 61, 62, 83, 85, 95, 137, 151, 174, 175, 181, 193
Sanctions for Evil iii, xv, 29, 173
Sanford, Nevitt iii, xvii, 9, 41, 145, 172, 191
Securing Our Planet iii, 29, 52, 182
sex xi, 44, 49, 51, 52, 53-56, 177
Shawn, Wallace (Wally) 13, 14, 16
Sheremetyevo xiv
simplicity 30, 34, 36, 37
social neutrino 43
Sovatsky, Stuart 53
"Soviets, Meet Middle America" 138, 139
spiritual xi, 50, 51, 53, 54, 60-63, 71, 73, 74, 76, 77, 86, 101, 159, 178, 179
Stanford 9, 10-12, 31, 34, 105, 174, 191
tantra xi, 49, 50, 53-57, 86, 177, 178
Tarcher, Jeremy (and his firm, Tarcher, Inc.) iii, 24, 52, 107, 114, 175, 177, 180, 182
teacher xi, xvii, 14, 24, 49, 50, 53, 57, 60, 61, 72, 74, 76, 85-92, 138, 146, 148, 152, 179, 182, 191
teleport 126
Tennison, Sharon 113, 137, 181, 183
Thanksgiving vi, 1-3
The Day After 103, 104, 180
The Fog of War 131-133

Thoreau, Henry David 28, 30 31-34, 36, 175, 176, 191
Tocqueville, Alexis de 114
Trafalgar Square 70, 113
Tuchman, Barbara 103, 180
Tunisia (North Africa) xix, 182
Turner, Ted 118, 119
TV xiv, 4-6, 13, 20, 43, 102-104, 114-117, 119, 124, 128, 138, 149, 161, 180, 192, 193
unconscious 27, 32, 43, 73, 86, 92, 152

useful idiot xiv
Veblen, Thorstein 31
von Bingen, Hildegaard 67
Walden 29-31, 36, 176
William James Center for Adult Development xi, 145, 171, 193
Worse Than Futile iii, 30, 176
Wright Institute xviii, 171
Yosemite 4, 34, 191
Zen 21, 71, 177, 182

Acknowledgements

My first thanks go to mentors, teachers, co-workers, and friends described in this book, including (in order of first appearance) a co-editor and co-worker Don Carlson; my parents, Marge and Roy Comstock; a mentor, the psychologist Nevitt Sanford; another mentor, the Harvard sociologist David Riesman; my siblings, Kani, Bruce, and Barbara; a friend and adviser at Stanford University, Yosal Rogat; the actress Shirley MacLaine; the spirit of Henry David Thoreau; my first client as a "book creation coach, the feminist Vicki Noble; my friend the tantrika Margo Anand (who now spells her first name with a final "t"); my brother-in-law the late Tibetologist Richard Kohn; Philip Glass (whom I know only through his music); Christina and Stan Grof (part of a circle important to me in the decade of this book and the next); the workshop founder Bob Hoffman; Soviets whom I met in what turned out to be the last years of the USSR; my fellow "peers" in the Elmwood Institute, especially Zenobia Barlow, the late Ernest (Chick) Callenbach and Chellis Glendinning.

I am also grateful to such early mentors as John U. Monro, dean of my college, whom I assisted in teaching a freshman seminar on expository prose; and to teachers who came after the decade described in this book but before it was written:

Angeles Arrien, who came from the Basque tradition, earned a doctorate in anthropology, and led us on a vision quest and through initiation rituals and performed a wedding in Yosemite; and my meditation teacher, Jun Po Dennis Kelly Roshi, with whom I studied in Ashland, Oregon.

Like my earlier book, *Gift of Darkness,* this book was proofread by Deborah Mokma, and designed and produced by Chris Molé, Book Savvy Studio. Once again, I am grateful for their professional eye and dedication.

Finally, I want to thank my wife, Shoshanah Dubiner. Apart from reviewing the graphic design of my books, among the recent projects of mine that she has supported in our "retirement" are advising on a series of more than seventy internet articles and a TV interview show that has so far produced more than one hundred half-hour episodes on "people doing admirable things," on people giving their gifts.

About the Author

A graduate of Harvard College, editor of the *Crimson* there, winner of the Frank Knox Fellowship for study abroad, Craig K. Comstock has worked mainly as co-director of the William James Center in Berkeley, then as a book creation coach with private clients, and also, for five years, as director of the Ark Foundation. After an adulthood largely in the San Francisco Bay Area, he now lives in southern Oregon, where he produces and hosts a weekly TV show on "people doing admirable things" and writes extensively for the internet. Author of several published books, he completed *Gift of Darkness: Growing Up in Occupied Amsterdam* in 2015.

www.ingramcontent.com/pod-product-compliance
Lightning Source LLC
Chambersburg PA
CBHW070144100426
42743CB00013B/2814